More Praise for *Change Your Questions, Change Your Life*

"The ideas in *Change Your Questions, Change Your Life* have had a profound impact on me and my business. Few books offer such potential to change *everything* in your work and life. Read this book and learn how to use the power of Question Thinking to revolutionize your thinking, solutions, and results."
  —Larina Kase, PsyD, MBA, author of *The Confident Leader* and
    coauthor of the *New York Times* bestseller *The Confident Speaker*

"Transformation, for individuals or organizations, always begins with new questions. Marilee Adams gives us simple yet incredibly powerful tools for finding our way to questions that change our lives."
  —Myron Rogers, coauthor of *A Simpler Way*

"In Congress or the physics lab, I focus on the important skill of asking myself the tough questions, framed in a way that they can be answered constructively. Marilee Adams's enlightening book teaches, in a skillful, readable way, techniques for asking the right questions so we can achieve preferred outcomes in our personal and professional lives—and also in how we can contribute as thoughtful citizens."
  —Rush Holt, U.S. Congressman

"Marilee Adams's insightful Question Thinking technology provides a precision of thought and inquiry that enables people to quickly get to the core of issues. We urgently need this kind of fresh approach to a 'transpartisan' perspective for dealing with the complex problems of our world. I strongly recommend her unique and powerful work."
  —Don Edward Beck, PhD, coauthor of *Spiral Dynamics*

"Well done, Dr. Adams. *Change Your Questions, Change Your Life* is the rare book that I use almost every day. I asked Learner questions to quickly transform a delicate organizational situation that had seemed intractable for a whole year. Your Question Thinking work changes paradigms, organizations, and lives. It's a classic!"
  —Rev. Dr. John McAuley, President and CEO, Muskoka Woods

"I really did love this book—and it's one of the most practical I've ever read. The greatest thing is that it's not a 'one and done' kind of book. You'll find yourself going back to it again and again. And you'll definitely find yourself sharing it with friends and colleagues. I know I have."
  —Tracy Davidson, Anchor and Consumer Reporter,
    NBC 10 News Philadelphia

W9-AUE-133

"Question Thinking offers patients, families, and clinicians a new paradigm for patient and relationship centered care. The simple yet profound framework of questions has the potential to contribute, at every level, to the transformation of heath care."

  —Cynda Hylton Rushton, PhD, RN, FAAN, Associate Professor, Nursing and Pediatrics, Johns Hopkins University School of Nursing, Robert Wood Johnson Executive Nurse Fellow

"We've used Question Thinking so successfully in our simulations that it led to a radical transformation in how people approach problems. It also made an immediate and sustained change in their behavior. In an organizational culture, the more people can be taught these processes, the greater positive impact it can have on productivity and the bottom line."

  —Carmella Granado, Senior Director of Organizational Effectiveness, Flextronics

"Marilee is smarter than anyone I know about asking the questions that really matter."

  —Lillian Brown, author of *Your Public Best* and *The Polished Politician*, named "one of the 100 most influential PR people of the century" by *PR Week*

"This book is great. I couldn't put it down! It clearly communicates how the questions we ask ourselves and others determine our results—and this makes all the difference for successful sales. I strongly recommend *Change Your Questions, Change Your Life* to everyone who takes my sales courses."

  —Jacques Werth, coauthor of *High Probability Selling*

"This book is an invitation to success for individuals and organizations. Dr. Marilee Adams has created a surprisingly simple and powerful practice for learning that propels us to our goals. Best of all, the same practices that make a difference for individuals also offer practical and impactful guidelines for learning organizations."

  —Victoria J. Marsick, PhD, Professor, Teachers College, Columbia University, and coauthor of *Sculpting the Learning Organization*

"A breath of fresh air. Of course, both questions and answers are necessary, but if you only focus on answers, the world becomes a very small place indeed. Marilee Adams helps open the door to innovation, creativity, and inspiration. This book is a treasure chest."

  —Harrison Owen, founder of Open Space Technology and author of *Wave Rider*

"This book may cause organizational leaders to take another look at their lists of competencies. If Question Thinking isn't already there, it may be time to go back to the drawing board. Marilee demonstrates why this capacity is absolutely essential to organizational and leadership success—and how easily it can be acquired."

— Beverly Kaye, PhD, coauthor of *Love 'Em or Lose 'Em* and *Love It, Don't Leave It*

"It was through the use of Dr. Adams's Question Thinking tools that I was able to help people reach a meaningful and successful resolution for a highly controversial project. Shifting from a Judger mentality to a solution-oriented one helped people move out of adversarial roles and enabled them to co-create a shared community."

— Tracey Pilkerton Cairnie, MS, Adjunct Professor, Conflict Analysis and Resolution, George Mason University

"Marilee's Question Thinking work shows us how to use questions to illuminate choices and help us understand how to manage our work and private lives in the most positive and productive ways. Marilee is a terrific presenter, and her workshops for our high-potential leaders made a significant and positive impact."

— Liz Barron, Director, Executive Leadership Programs, The Brookings Institution

"This fable is destined to be a classic in the Og Mandino genre. Question Thinking will make your life more effective regardless of personal history, personality type, or profession. Buy this book and read it tonight. Your life will never be the same."

— Stewart Levine, author of *The Book of Agreement* and *Getting to Resolution*

"*Change Your Questions, Change Your Life* is an amazing conversation. With clarity and accessibility, Marilee models a process whereby we can intentionally change our way of internal inquiry. Imagine being in conscious charge of our own thoughts! A wonderful tool for coaches, helping professionals, and all who desire to transform their inner conversations."

— Pamela Richarde, Master Certified Coach, Past President, International Coach Federation

"Question Thinking is brilliant and simple. Marilee demonstrates how you can use the power of questions to transform any and every area of your life. By changing your questions you are able to transform the way you think, the way you act, and importantly, the results you can achieve. This book is an ideal guide for anyone looking for positive results at work or at home."

— Lori Sheppard, President, EDGEucation Worldwide Enterprises

change
your
questions
change
your life

Inquiry Institute Library Series

change your questions

change your life

10 powerful tools for life and work

Second Edition

Marilee Adams, Ph.D.

BK

Berrett–Koehler Publishers, Inc.
San Francisco
a BK Life book

Berrett-Koehler Publishers, Inc.
1333 Broadway, Suite 1000
Oakland, CA 94612-1921
Tel: (510) 817-2277   Fax: (510) 817-2278   www.bkconnection.com

Ordering Information

Quantity sales. Special discounts are available on quantity purchases by corporations, associations, and others. For details, contact the "Special Sales Department" at the Berrett-Koehler address above.
Individual sales. Berrett-Koehler publications are available through most bookstores. They can also be ordered directly from Berrett-Koehler: Tel: (800) 929-2929; Fax: (802) 864-7626; www.bkconnection.com
Orders for college textbook/course adoption use. Please contact Berrett-Koehler: Tel: (800) 929-2929; Fax: (802) 864-7626.
Orders by U.S. trade bookstores and wholesalers. Please contact Ingram Publisher Services, Tel: (800) 509-4887; Fax: (800) 838-1149; E-mail: customer.service@ingrampublisherservices.com; or visit www.ingrampublisherservices.com/Ordering for details about electronic ordering.

Berrett-Koehler and the BK logo are registered trademarks of Berrett-Koehler Publishers, Inc.

Printed in the United States of America

Berrett-Koehler books are printed on long-lasting acid-free paper. When it is available, we choose paper that has been manufactured by environmentally responsible processes. These may include using trees grown in sustainable forests, incorporating recycled paper, minimizing chlorine in bleaching, or recycling the energy produced at the paper mill.

Library of Congress Cataloging-in-Publication Data
Adams, Marilee G., 1945-
   Change your questions, change your life : 10 powerful tools for life and work / Marilee Adams. — 2nd ed.

158.1

   p. cm.
   Includes bibliographical references.
   ISBN 978-1-57675-600-3 (pbk. : alk. paper)
   1. Change (Psychology)   2. Self-talk.   I. Title.
   BF637.C4A33 2009
   158.1—dc22   2009008709

Second Edition
20 19 18 17 16 15 14   20 19 18 17 16 15 14 13 12 11

The Choice Map on pp. 38–39, and the Switching Lanes graphic on page 75 are both copyright © 1998 by John Wiley & Sons.

Design and production: Detta Penna; Copyediting: Patricia Brewer; Proofreading: Katherine Lee; Cover design: Mark van Bronkhorst, MvB Design.

For Ed Adams,
my husband and muse

Contents

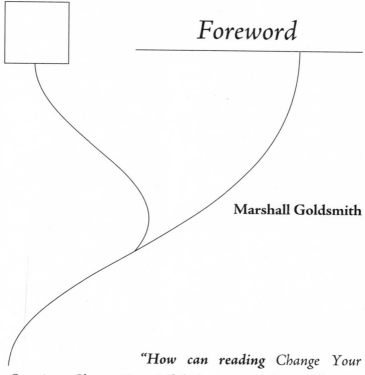

Foreword

Marshall Goldsmith

"How can reading Change Your Questions, Change Your Life help you and the people who are important to you have better lives?" This is the key question I urge you to keep in mind as you read this valuable book. The great ideas presented here, in a system of tools Marilee Adams calls *Question Thinking,* provide a solid new way of thinking that can make a positive difference in all our lives.

There are many ideas in this book that helped me. You're sure to find some that will help you, too. *Change Your Questions, Change Your Life* provides methods, skills, and tools for easily implementing Question Thinking both at home and at work. To begin with, Marilee shows how we can become more effective and efficient by focusing on learning rather than judging. As a Buddhist, I know this is key to having a happier, more productive life.

Marilee shows us the power of questions to direct our thinking, and therefore our actions and results. This means that we can intentionally affect the future by designing the most powerful questions for getting us there. That's what great coaching is all about. It's also what great leaders do — they provide us with visions of new futures. Marilee offers question tools for both coaches and leaders to optimize and fulfill their missions.

It's no surprise that *Change Your Questions, Change Your Life* became a bestseller. It made so much of a real difference in people's lives that they shared the book with their teams and their companies and also with their families and friends. The story in the Introduction says it all — a reader wrote Marilee that he used the methods in the book so successfully that his company got a mention in *Inc. Magazine.* That's also why so many coaches use the Question Thinking methods and also give the book to their coachees.

In my mission as an executive coach, I help successful leaders get better measurable results. This includes teaching a process called feed*forward.* Leaders learn to ask for ideas to move the future. They refine their ability to listen without judgment and to say "thank you" for suggestions. Marilee would call this "Learner listening." This is invaluable for all coaches, leaders, and managers.

Racecar drivers are taught to "focus on the road — not the wall." As you read this book, focus on the road that represents your highest potential by asking questions that lead to a better future, such as "What are the greatest positive possibilities I can imagine?"

The second edition delivers even more than the first. The new chapters and tools make the material even more accessible and practical. *Change Your Questions, Change Your Life* has great wisdom for us all. Take it very seriously. Roll up your sleeves and get to work. The best way to get the most *out* of this book is to practice everything *in* it!

Life is good!

Marshall Goldsmith

Author, *What Got You Here Won't Get You There*

Winner of the Harold Longman Award
as the Best Business Book of 2007

Named by the American Management Association
as one of 50 great thinkers and leaders influencing
the field of management over the past 80 years

Introduction

One summer afternoon, shortly after the first edition of this book was published, I answered my office phone to hear a man's booming voice announce, "You don't know me, but I'm Ben." He laughed, and I laughed along with him because I knew exactly what he was referring to. Ben is the main character in *Change Your Questions, Change Your Life,* and this caller identified with him so much that he thought I could also help him and his organization.

By now, Ben is almost legendary for many of my readers. Proud of being the "Answer Man," he believes he must always have the answers and must always be right. In the

1

story — a business fable through which readers experience the practical power of *Question Thinking* — Ben is floundering in his new leadership position. But that isn't all. He's also having trouble at home. His relationship with Grace, his wife of less than a year, is growing increasingly tense. When we first meet him, Ben is one unhappy guy.

Since that first telephone call from a "Ben," I've received many similar messages from both men and women. One reader, David, wrote me that like Ben, he'd been in trouble at work, especially with his team. After reading *Change Your Questions* he changed his own questions and, in the process, changed his leadership style. He was ultimately so successful that the results were included in an article in *Inc. Magazine*. You'll find the reference for that article in the notes at the end of this book.

Change Your Questions has struck a chord with so many readers that it has become a bestseller. The first inkling I had of its impact occurred when the senior manager at a large pharmaceutical company called me with an invitation to a discussion group featuring my book. She had sent copies to the 50 members of her globally dispersed team with just one instruction: "Come to the book discussion with one example of *something you've done differently* as a result of reading this book." On the day of the meeting I was ushered into a conference room with about thirty people seated around a large table. Others joined us by speakerphone. I listened in amazement as person after person described the results they'd achieved. One man told us he was leading his team more successfully, a woman shared that her relationship with a direct report had improved significantly, and a plant manager in Brazil explained how reading the book helped him recognize and correct a problem in his plant.

Since then, I've given results-focused Question Thinking presentations at some of the world's largest corporations, at major federal agencies, at nonprofits, and in communities. Largely through word of mouth, *Change Your Questions* has become required reading in leadership development programs, executive coach trainings, and college courses. It is used by teams in companies and government agencies, by health care professionals in major hospitals, and by Human Resource professionals as well as those in sales. It's used in church-sponsored marriage enrichment workshops, in decision-making programs in prisons, and as part of creativity and innovation initiatives in organizations large and small. Community leaders have used it to find constructive responses to tough challenges in inner cities. Coaches and mediators give it to their clients. People share it with their partners, their adult and teenage children, and their friends and colleagues.

One might wonder why *Change Your Questions* has gained such widespread traction. Question Thinking (QT), the heart of the book, takes on an age-old issue — our ability to be in charge of our own thinking, moment by moment by moment. QT provides skills for observing and assessing our present thinking—including the questions we're asking ourselves—and then guides us in designing new questions for getting better results. In other words, QT helps us think productively rather than reactively, and to choose wisely rather than simply react. Building such a reliable capacity for thinking is central to the skills required for intentional and sustainable change, whether that change is sought in our professional or personal lives. Without these skills, our goals for change may be only wistful slogans that will never come to fruition.

Question Thinking began with an important moment of discovery in my own life. I was a determined young graduate student working away on my Ph.D. dissertation. Not only did I endure a ruthless inner critic, but criticisms from others often left me in tears. One fateful day, expecting high praise from my advisor for some work I felt great about, I instead heard from him, "Marilee, this is just not acceptable." At that moment something new happened. Instead of tearfully wondering what was wrong with me, I took a deep breath, and becoming calm and curious, simply asked him, "OK, how do I fix it?" That simple shift took me from feeling powerless to being confident enough to take constructive action. Afterward I wondered, *Could this seeming miracle be turned into a reliable method for myself and others?* And so I began.

In spite of its power for bringing about genuine, sustainable change, the tools and skills of Question Thinking are both simple and practical. Readers say that QT provides a natural "how to" they find missing in many books on business and personal development. Again and again, readers like David tell me that Ben's story succeeds in showing them how to make real changes so that their own lives are distinctly different and better. Nothing could be more satisfying to an author!

The material in this book aligns well with other philosophies and systems for change such as Appreciative Inquiry, Positive Psychology, and Emotional Intelligence (EQ). I've given Question Thinking workshops for groups that employ Action Learning programs and in companies committed to becoming better learning organizations. I've talked about it on radio and television. I've also presented this work to my peers in many professional associations, including the American Society for Training and Development, the International Coach Federation, the Organizational Development Network, and the Society for Human Resource Managers.

Readers and people in those audiences resonate with the core message of Question Thinking — that *real change always begins with a change in thinking* — and most specifically in the questions we ask ourselves. Stories like this one about Susan help them understand how practical and specific this can be. Susan was a participant in one of my corporate Inquiry Workshops and asked for help with a dilemma at work. She loved her work, but conflicts with her boss left her wondering if she should quit her job. When I asked what questions she was asking herself about him, she replied, with an edge to her voice, "What's he going to do wrong *now?*" and "How's he going to make *me* look bad?" Clearly, whatever the source of the conflict, Susan's current thinking would render any satisfying resolution nearly impossible.

I realized that Susan needed to change her questions if she wanted a better result. When I suggested a new one for her to ask herself — "What can *I* do to make my boss look *good?*" — she looked completely startled. This question was clearly outside the mindset with which Susan had been viewing her boss! Even so, she agreed to give it a try.

When I ran into Susan and her husband months later, she gave me a huge smile and asked if I wanted to hear about the "miracles" that had occurred at work since we had talked. "I kept my job *and* got a promotion and a raise," she reported proudly. "But the most amazing thing is that my boss and I volunteered to work on a committee together, even though we used to avoid being in the same room. And it turned out great." Then Susan's husband commented that the positive changes had not all been at work. Smiling at his wife he explained, "*My* life is easier since Susan stopped complaining about her boss every night!"

While *Change Your Questions, Change Your Life* is a business fable, its impact is much broader than the world of work. You will find, just as Ben — and Susan — did, that the same principles that are so successful in business situations can also help us greatly improve relationships in our personal lives.

Ted, a senior engineer attending an Inquiring Leadership workshop at a Fortune 100 company, took seriously my assignment to practice switching from being judgmental to taking a creative learning attitude. The result? That night at dinner he and his 16-year-old son had their best conversation in over a year. The next morning Ted told us, "My son has an uncanny ability to 'push my buttons,' and usually my reaction is like what you call a Judger hijacking. But last night was totally different. I didn't take the bait, didn't yell at him and we didn't end up in a fight like we usually do." Ted looked quite pleased with himself as he mentioned that his son had smiled, rolled his eyes, and quipped, "What happened to *you*?!"

When my publisher asked me to write a second edition of *Change Your Questions, Change Your Life*, I saw it as a wonderful opportunity to add new material that my clients and workshop participants have found particularly helpful. Some chapters have new titles and there are also some new chapters: "We're All Recovering Judgers" (You can laugh at this truth — others do, too!), "Learner Teams and Judger Teams," and "Q-Storming to the Rescue." In addition, there are new tools in the Question Thinking Tools Section following Ben's story.

In my first book, *The Art of the Question*, I wrote that "questions are like treasures hidden in broad daylight." My goal with *Change Your Questions, Change Your Life* is to provide an easy-to-follow map so you can quickly find that treasure and make it your own. I also use storytelling to make it possible for readers to experience what Question Thinking can bring to their lives. Questions open our minds, our eyes, and our hearts. With them, we learn, connect, and create. And with them, we can create better futures and better results. I hope that Ben's story shows you, in a practical way, how a world of questions really can lead to those kinds of possibilities.

There are many important implications in exploring the territory I've termed Question Thinking. For example, imagine the difference these perspectives and tools could make in education, in parenting, and in health care. We might even wonder, "What might taking a Question Thinking perspective make possible for us as human beings who yearn to create positive futures for ourselves as individuals, families, organizations, and our world?"

I have a vision of workplaces and a society — of individuals, families, institutions, and communities — that are vibrant with the spirit of inquiry. Our orientation would shift from one of fixed opinions and easy answers to one of curiosity and thoughtful questions. This is the path that lights the way for open-minded and successful collaboration, for exploration, discovery, and innovation — and for the real possibility of a desirable future for us all.

Now it's time to meet Ben and discover, along with him, how changing your questions really can change your life.

Moment of Truth

A rosewood paperweight on my desk bears a sterling silver plaque declaring: *Great results begin with great questions.* It was a gift from a very special person in my life — Joseph S. Edwards — who introduced me to Question Thinking, or QT, as he called the skills he taught me. QT opened up a part of my mind that otherwise I might never have discovered. Like everyone else, I believed the way to fix a problem was to look for the right answers. Instead, Joseph showed me that the best way to solve a problem is to *first* come up with better questions. The skills he taught me rescued my career and saved my marriage as well. Both were definitely in trouble at the time.

It all started when I was invited to take a position at QTec. The company was in the midst of a major overhaul at the time, and the word on the street was that, barring a miracle, they would fold before the year was out. A friend warned me that accepting a position with QTec would be like signing up on a sinking ship. What convinced me to take the risk? It was my trust in Alexa Harte, the recently appointed CEO at QTec, who'd offered me the position. I'd worked with her for years at KB Corp, my previous employer, where she'd won my respect as a gifted leader. Her confidence about turning QTec around was infectious. Besides, she promised me a great promotion: hefty pay raise, impressive title, and a chance to act as lead in developing an innovative new product. If everything went well the risk would pay off in aces. If not...well, I tried not to think about that.

At first I was riding high, convinced I had the job wired. Alexa had hired me for my engineering smarts and I knew I could deliver on that count. The new product really intrigued me and the technical challenges were right up my alley. At KB — where Alexa said she'd seen me work miracles — I'd won accolades as the Answer Guy. I'd faced down the toughest technical problems, one right after the other. However, at QTec I was also facing a different kind of challenge — leading a team. I was sure that would be simple even though Alexa let me know I'd have to put effort into developing my people and management skills.

My team seemed an enthusiastic and talented bunch

and for a while everything went great. Then life at work started unraveling. It was as if suddenly a glaring spotlight was focused on my shortcomings. I didn't dare say it, but secretly I decided I'd been stuck with a bunch of losers.

To make matters worse, there was Charles. Before I came aboard at QTec he'd been passed over for the job I'd been offered. I could understand why he might resent me. And, just as I expected, he was a real troublemaker from the word go, questioning everything I said and did.

Things went from bad to worse. Our ship was sinking and I couldn't figure out how to plug up the leaks. Team meetings were a farce — no discussions, no solutions. And nobody had to remind me that if we couldn't get our product to market before the competition, we would prove the naysayers right.

Life wasn't much better at home. Tension was growing with Grace, my wonderful wife of less than eight months. She constantly asked me about what was going on at work. Finally, one day I just told her she was asking too many questions and she should keep her nose out of my business. She was hurt, I was miserable, and I hadn't the vaguest idea what to do about it.

I didn't want Grace to know how much difficulty I was having. I'd always taken great pride in solving problems that baffled everyone else. This time, with any luck, the right answers would turn up before Grace, Alexa, and the people on my team found out the job was way over my head.

Meanwhile I kept more and more to myself and did my best to just get through each day.

I was mystified and overwhelmed. It seemed like everything in my life was falling apart. Then came the awful turning point. Grace and I had an argument in the morning and only hours later there was a major crisis at work. Nobody said it, but I could see it in their eyes: We were cooked. It was my moment of truth.

I needed to be alone and face facts. I called Grace and left a message that I'd be putting in an all-nighter to finish an important report. Then I spent the whole long night in my office, staring at the walls, still searching desperately for the right answers, and reliving the most disastrous weeks of my life. I told myself I had to face the truth; I had failed. Just after six that morning I went out for coffee and then started drafting my resignation. I finished three hours later, called Alexa, and made arrangements to see her immediately.

The walk to Alexa's suite was less than a hundred yards. That morning it felt like a hundred miles. When I got to the big double doors of her office I stopped and took a deep breath to regain my composure. I stood there for some long moments, working up the nerve to knock. Just as I was raising my arm, I heard a voice behind me.

"Ben Knight, you're here. Good, good!"

It was Alexa. There was no mistaking that voice, always cheerful, exuding a sense of optimism even when things were going badly. An attractive, athletic-looking woman in her early fifties, she radiated confidence. I told Grace that I'd never met anyone quite like Alexa. She approached her responsibilities at QTec with boundless enthusiasm. It wasn't that she didn't take her job seriously. She did that in spades! But she did it with such pleasure and self-assurance that she made it look easy.

At that moment, her mere presence made me acutely aware of my own deficiencies. I felt numb, barely mumbling a subdued good morning as she touched my shoulder and ushered me into her office.

The room was expansive, the size of a large living room in the best executive home. I crossed deep green carpeting, soft underfoot, and walked over to the large bay window where the meeting area was set up. There, two overstuffed sofas faced one another across a large walnut coffee table.

"Sit!" Alexa said, gesturing in a welcoming way to one of the couches. "Betty said your lights were on when she left her office at seven-thirty last night, and you were here when she came in early this morning."

She sat down across from me on the other couch.

"I presume that's for me?" Alexa asked, pointing to the green folder containing my resignation that I'd placed on the coffee table.

I nodded, waiting for her to pick it up. Instead, she leaned back, looking as if she had all the time in the world.

"Tell me what's going on with you," she said.

I pointed to the green folder. "It's my resignation. I'm sorry, Alexa."

The next sound I heard stopped me cold. It was not a gasp, not a word of reproach, but laughter! It was not cruel laughter, either. What had I missed? I didn't understand. How could Alexa still sound sympathetic in the face of all I'd screwed up?

"Ben," she said, "you're not going to quit on me." She slid the folder in my direction. "Take this back. I know more about your situation than you realize. I want you to give me at least six more weeks. But for that period of time, you've got to commit to making changes."

"Are you sure about this?" I asked, dumbfounded.

"Let me answer you this way," she continued. "Many years ago, I was in a situation similar to yours. I had to face facts. If I wanted to be successful I'd need to make some fundamental changes. I was pretty desperate. A man by the name of Joseph sat me down and asked some straightforward questions, simple ones on the surface. But those questions opened doors I never even knew existed. He asked, 'Are you willing to take responsibility for your mistakes — and for the attitudes and actions that led to them?' Then he said, 'Are you willing — however begrudgingly — to forgive yourself, and even laugh at yourself?' And finally, 'Will you look for value in your experiences, especially the most difficult ones?' Bottom line, 'Are you willing to learn from what happened and make changes accordingly?' "

She went on to tell me how Joseph's work changed not only her life but her husband Stan's as well. "Stan has tripled his income in the past few years. He attributes the success he and his company enjoy today to what Joseph taught him. Joseph would tell you all about it. He loves to tell stories, especially ones about how people's lives were changed by changing their questions."

I must have looked perplexed because she added, "Don't worry about what I mean by *questions that change people's lives*. You'll learn about that soon enough." She paused. Then, in carefully measured words, she said, "I want you to work with my friend Joseph, starting immediately. I'm sure he'll want to meet with you a number of times. Figure out the schedule with him. This is top priority now."

"What is he, a therapist?" The idea of seeing a shrink made me nervous.

Alexa smiled. "No, he's an executive coach. I call him an *inquiring coach*."

Inquiring coach! If I knew anything at all, it was that I needed answers, not more questions. What good could more questions possibly be to me?

As I left, Alexa jotted something down and sealed it in an envelope. "Inside this envelope is a prediction I've made," she said mysteriously, handing it to me. "Put it in that green folder of yours and don't open it until you've completed your work with Joseph." Then she gave me his business card. I turned it over. There was a big question mark on the other side. It really irritated me. The idea that I'd be spending valuable time with a man whose logo was a question mark went against everything I believed.

Back in my own office, I collapsed in the chair behind my desk. My eyes fell on a small gilded frame on the wall. It held a saying, just two words long: *Question everything!* It was a quote attributed to Albert Einstein. Many rooms at QTec contained a framed placard exactly like this one. As much as I respected and appreciated Alexa's leadership, this had always been a point of contention for me. Leaders should have *answers*, not questions.

I was still holding Joseph's card with the question mark on the back. What had I gotten myself into? Only time would tell. At least I could put off my decision to resign. My attention shifted to Grace. How was I ever going to smooth things over with her? At that moment there was only one thing to be grateful for — Alexa hadn't asked about Grace and me. I think that would have been the last straw. I knew Alexa was fond of my wife — she'd even come to our wedding. She wouldn't have been happy to find out we were having trouble.

I sat there for a long time just staring at Joseph's card. The fact that Alexa had refused to accept my resignation offered a little hope. I was encouraged that she would refer me to her own mentor. Even though the jury was still out on whether her trust in me was deserved, I had nothing to lose by keeping an appointment with this inquiring coach guy. Besides, even though I was skeptical, I was also curious. If this Joseph had helped Alexa and Stan so much, maybe he had answers that would help me too.

> # Question everything!

2   *A Challenge Accepted*

My appointment with Joseph S. Edwards was at ten the next morning. I didn't tell Grace about this meeting nor about my conversation with Alexa. And I certainly didn't tell her about writing my resignation. Admitting I was in trouble had never come easy for me. For weeks now I'd been stonewalling Grace and feeling more and more resentful about all her questions. Until I found the right answers and solutions I was determined to tough it out and keep my problems to myself. But as usually happened with Grace, I wasn't so good at hiding my problems.

I should have realized she knew something more than

the usual job stress was bothering me. That morning, on our way to the airport where Grace was catching a plane for a lunch meeting in another city, she brought things to a head. As I pulled up to the curb at the terminal, she told me, "I've been feeling like a widow lately. You've been so distant and moody. Ben, if you want a real partnership with me, you're going to have to make some changes."

God knows I love Grace but I wasn't in the best of moods.

"I don't need this right now," I told her, more harshly than I intended.

Grace looked stunned. I got out of the car to get her briefcase from the trunk. As I handed it to her our eyes met, and for a moment I was afraid she was going to cry. I knew it wasn't right leaving her like that, but I was feeling pushed. Besides, if I got dragged into a long discussion, I'd be late for my appointment with Joseph. Our little problem would have to wait. Grace forced a smile, told me she'd be back that night, but not to worry about picking her up. She'd get the express shuttle home. She turned and quickly disappeared into the crowd.

I was angry. *Why did she have to choose this particular morning to pick a fight?* I hit the accelerator and pulled out into traffic. Horns blasted. I slammed on my brakes as some maniac raced by, barely missing me. I was fuming. Between that near collision, the conflict with Grace, and having to attend a meeting I dreaded, my morning was off to a very bad start.

Chapter 2

Joseph's office was in the Pearl Building downtown, a fourteen-story edifice constructed in the 1930s and recently restored. Old Town, as we called the area, was a bustling shopping center with great places to eat and drink, and unusual little stores. Grace and I often had dinner there, at a small place called the Metropol. Grace is an art lover, and she'd opened up a whole new world I'd hardly known existed. Thanks to her, we'd spent many happy hours together, browsing through bookstores and art galleries. Passing our familiar haunts that morning, I worried about what the future held for us.

I pushed open the polished brass-framed doors at the Pearl Building, crossed the marble floors, and caught an elevator to Joseph's penthouse office. I stepped into a large foyer that looked like someone's private residence. Several tall ficus trees reached up toward a large skylight.

Beyond this private anteroom, a double set of doors opened invitingly. A long hallway stretched beyond them. On its walls hung some kind of artwork. I remember thinking that Grace would enjoy seeing this.

"You must be Ben Knight!" Joseph Edwards strode rapidly toward me, greeting me enthusiastically. I judged him to be in his early 60s, though he moved like an agile sprinter a quarter that age. No more than 5 feet 9, he was dressed casually, with an outrageous sweater knit with a myriad of striped patterns that dazzled the eye.

Joseph's smooth-shaven face glowed with good humor. His brown eyes sparkled with excitement, almost childlike.

Atop his head, a wild array of woolly white curls reminded me of photos I'd seen of Albert Einstein in his later years.

Joseph's warm welcome dissolved some of my reservations about spending time with him. He led me down the hallway to his office, explaining as we went that the walls displayed "some artifacts I call my *Question Thinking Hall of Fame*." What I had mistaken for works of art were instead framed magazine articles and letters. We turned left into a large room bathed in the morning sunlight.

The room contained comfortable seating, a well-used brick fireplace, and a walnut conference table with matching chairs. One wall displayed certificates and a few dozen autographed photos, many with their subjects shaking hands with Joseph. In the pictures I recognized faces I'd seen in the news over the years. Alexa hadn't quite prepared me for this. Joseph was obviously very well connected in the business world and beyond.

I also saw covers of three different books displayed in elegant frames. They were all written by Joseph. Each had the words *Question Thinking* in the title. One in particular caught my eye. It was co-authored with a Sarah Edwards and was about inquiring marriages.

I was impressed but also intimidated. We entered a less formal room, where I felt slightly more at ease. Windows on three sides afforded a spectacular view of the city. In the distance, wispy clouds were lifting from the woods. The views seemed to stretch on forever.

I eased myself into a large leather armchair while Joseph took his place near me in a matching one. He dangled a pair of rimless reading glasses from his left hand.

After some brief get-acquainted conversation, he asked, "Tell me, what do you suppose is your greatest asset?"

"I'm the *Answer Man*, the *Go-To* guy," I told him with pride. "I've built my whole career around being the person people go to for answers. The bottom line for me is answers. That's what business is all about."

"True. But how can you get the best answers without the best questions?" Joseph paused, placing his glasses on his nose and peering over the top of them at me: "Is there a single question you would say characterizes the way you operate?"

"Sure," I said. "Get the right answers and be ready to back them up, that's my motto."

Joseph asked me to restate that as a question, one I would ask myself. I couldn't see the point, but I did as he asked, "Okay. Sure. The question I operate with is, *How can I prove I'm right?*"

"That's great," Joseph said. "Then we might have your problem nailed already."

"My problem?"

"Being the Answer Man. Having to prove you're right," Joseph said. "I must say, Ben, we're getting down to business faster than I expected."

I wasn't sure if I'd heard him correctly. *Was he kidding?* No, he was dead serious. "I beg your pardon?"

"Finding proof that our answers are correct can be important," he said. "But would you allow that there are times when too much of a good thing can get you in trouble? For example, how do you think your having to be right all the time goes over with your team?"

"I'm not sure what you mean," I said, and I really meant it. I wanted my team to find answers, the correct answers. "Everyone's looking for answers." That's what we all got paid to do, wasn't it?

"Let me get personal for a moment," Joseph said. "Do your efforts to prove you're right work with your wife?"

That one hit home. "Not really," I admitted reluctantly. Grace had told me how my habit of insisting on being right often frustrated her.

"It doesn't work so well with my wife either," Joseph said smiling. "With that in mind, let's look a little deeper into what questions really do. Certainly we recognize that questions are a vital part of communication. But the role they play in thinking is not always obvious, and that's where Question Thinking skills can be invaluable.

"If you're willing to grab onto the real power of questions, they can change your whole life. It comes down to increasing the quantity and quality of the questions we ask ourselves and each other. It also matters enormously where we're coming from when we ask those questions."

I must have looked puzzled because Joseph paused

and said, "You've never heard the term *Question Thinking* before, have you?"

I shook my head, no.

"*Question Thinking* is a system of skills and tools using questions to expand how you approach virtually any situation. You develop the skills to refine your questions for vastly better results in anything you do. The QT system can literally put action into your thinking — action that's both focused and effective. It's a great way to create a foundation for making wiser choices."

"Go on," I said, skeptically.

"Much of the time we're barely conscious of asking questions, especially the ones we ask ourselves. But they're a part of our thought process nearly every moment of our lives. Thinking actually occurs as an internal question and answer process. Not only that, we often answer our own questions by taking some action.

"Here's an example. When you got dressed this morning, I'll bet you went to your closet, or dresser — or maybe even the floor — and asked yourself questions like: *Where am I going? What's the weather? What's comfortable?* Or even, *What's clean?* You answered your questions by *doing* something. You selected some clothing and put it on. You are, in effect, wearing your answers."

"I guess I can't argue with that. As you say, though, if I did ask those questions, I hardly noticed at the time.

Actually, my biggest question was whether Grace picked up my suit at the cleaners, like she promised."

We both laughed.

> **Question Thinking** is a system of tools for transforming thinking, action, and results through skillful question asking—questions we ask ourselves as well as those we ask others.

I could tell Joseph was getting on a roll. I decided to just sit back and hear him out.

"When we get stuck, it's natural to go on a hunt for answers and solutions. But in doing so we often unintentionally create blocks instead of openings. To solve our problems, we *first* need to change our questions; otherwise we'll probably just keep getting the same old answers, over and over again.

"New questions can totally shift our perspectives, moving us into fresh ways of looking at problems. Questions have even changed the course of history. Let me give you a dramatic example. Think about this. Long ago, nomadic societies were driven by the implicit question, *How do we get ourselves to water?*"

I nodded. "Which is what kept them nomadic...."

"Yet look what happened when their implicit question changed to, *How do we get water to come to us?* That new question initiated one of humanity's most significant paradigm shifts. It ushered in agriculture, including the invention of irrigation, the storage of water, digging wells, cultivation, and eventually the creation of cities."

"I guess I can see how questions apply to getting dressed and even to that paradigm shift for the nomads. But how does this apply to business? And more to the point, how can it help *me* with my situation at work?"

"The point is that *questions drive results*," Joseph responded. "They virtually program how we behave and what kinds of outcomes are possible. Consider three companies, each one driven by one of the following questions: *What's the best way to satisfy shareholders? What's the best way to satisfy customers? What's the best way to satisfy employees?* Each question takes your mind in a different direction in terms of a business. Each will have a different influence on priorities, everyday behavior, and strategies for achieving goals. Remember: *Questions drive results*. That's as true in your day to day life at QTec as it was for nomads thousands of years ago."

Questions drive results.

"Your ideas are interesting," I hedged. "But I've literally built my reputation on having answers...not questions."

"Fortunately," Joseph continued, "the route from being

an Answer Man to becoming a Question Man is much shorter than you might think."

What was he suggesting? Giving up my cherished role as the Answer Man was about the furthest thing from my mind. I wasn't about to give up something that had worked so well for me for so long. One thing I was pretty certain of — if we'd only stuck with questions, we'd still be scratching our heads and hunting for our suppers with pointed sticks.

Joseph removed his glasses and paused, as if contemplating what he was going to say next. Then he spoke in a slow, even voice.

"Ben, you've got to face facts here — you're in trouble. One of your greatest assets — being the Answer Man — has turned into a liability. That's the bottom line."

As Joseph spoke, I imagined Grace sitting here in Joseph's office with me. Truly, she would applaud what he was saying. A big knot tightened in my belly.

"If being the Answer Man were still working for you," Joseph continued, "you wouldn't have spent the night in your office writing your resignation. Alexa told me about that. I know where you were coming from. I've had my own share of all-night debates with the walls of my office.

"This is where I think I can help you," he said. "Alexa has been watching your career for a long time. She believes you've got great potential, and she's obviously invested a lot in you. But she also thinks that without some big changes you won't make it at QTec. She knows you pretty well, Ben. Before she hired you she shared her concerns with me about bringing you into the company. If I'm not mistaken, she also told you what she was worried about. Alexa is not exactly a shrinking violet."

We both laughed at that comment, and I was grateful for a moment of levity. Alexa was about the most forthright human being I'd ever met. She never beat around the bush.

With more than a little embarrassment, I remembered her exact words the day she hired me: "Ben, I'm bringing you in because you're absolutely the best in your field. I'm completely confident about your technical acumen, which we need for the new markets we plan to open up. What I'm not as comfortable with is your people skills. That's where you need to improve if you're going to make it as a leader. I'm gambling on you, but I plan on winning this bet."

At the time, I had brushed off Alexa's warning. Instead, I had immediately called Grace to tell her about my great *coup*. If I'd heard Alexa's warning at all, it was filtered through the plans I was making for a victory celebration with Grace that evening.

"As an Answer Man," Joseph said, "your dogged determination to find the right answers has led you to some brilliant breakthroughs. However, the line between having the right answers and being perceived as a know-it-all is a thin one, indeed. You could even come off as arrogant and uncaring. My guess is that with the added pressure and responsibility of your new position, that know-it-all style has gotten exaggerated. Once you get labeled, you're in trouble. When others start seeing you that way, can you really expect them to like you? It's not exactly an ideal leadership profile."

"Who's running a popularity contest here?" I countered. In my mind, a good leader has one responsibility — get the job done and see that others follow through on their assignments. Nobody on my team was producing.

"Whenever you're interacting with other people as a leader," Joseph said, "you want them to take initiative, ask questions, and come up with answers that maybe you hadn't thought of yourself. Your accomplishments come from the total efforts of the people you're working with, not just from your own solitary work."

Joseph went to his desk and took something from the side drawer. As he handed it to me I read the title: *Question Thinking Workbook*. I began flipping through the pages.

"If it's true that you're coming across as a know-it-all," he continued, "which is the downfall of the Answer Man, you don't leave much room for anyone else. You're great at the technical stuff, Ben, but your present job requires much more than that. You're working with people, not objects. Where people are concerned, there's a certain magic in getting just the right mixture between questions and answers. I can offer this suggestion: Start by asking more and telling a lot less. The most effective communication is usually far more about asking and less about telling. How else can you make room for new information from other people? Conventional wisdom has it turned around — 80 percent telling and 20 percent asking. Ben, it's vital for you to ask more questions — not just about technical matters but about people. Questions like, *What can I do to get people more engaged and working together effectively?*"

"Seems to me you're overemphasizing questions," I said. "Everyone has questions, that's a no-brainer. But it's the guy with answers who makes things happen."

"Face it, Ben, you've hit a wall. Are you going to climb over it? Alexa is convinced you will. It's your choice, not mine, so I can't answer that question for you. However, here are some questions you might ask yourself: *Do I listen to people's questions and suggestions? Do people feel respected by me? Do I encourage others to take initiative, ask questions, and contribute their own ideas?*

"You look perplexed," Joseph said. "Want to share what's going on with you?"

I was taken aback by his question. I hadn't expected this meeting to get so personal. This people skills stuff was making me uncomfortable. "All this theory might be fine," I said. "But the only question I care about is how do I *apply* what you're telling me? We've got to get down to brass tacks, not just thinking and asking questions. These meetings with you have to be practical or — what's the point?

"You and I have very different ways of thinking. You

31

A Challenge Accepted

think in questions. I think in answers. You're going to have to prove to me that this Question Thinking of yours can be practical enough to make a difference with my problems."

"Fair enough," Joseph said, thoughtfully. "Let's start with another question: Would you agree that you're looking for ways to change?"

I shrugged. "Isn't the fact that I'm here proof enough that I'm looking for changes?"

"In order to change something, you need a good way to understand where you're starting from. The better you can *observe* that, the more effective you'll be with making the changes you want. And that's where Question Thinking can help you. Really effective, intentional change begins with strengthening your *observer self*. The better you can see what's already there — that's where the observer self comes in — the better you can apply the right skills and strategies to make the changes you want."

Joseph's emphasis on the observer self piqued my interest. I was familiar with using this observer part of myself to solve technical problems by questioning what was working, what wasn't working, and coming up with answers to solve a problem. But I had never looked through that same lens when it came to how I interacted with people around me.

"There's a section in the workbook on becoming a better observer," Joseph said. "That's the first tool. Please read it over and think about it before we meet again."

I nodded absently as I searched for the place he was

talking about in the workbook. Ready or not, the self-observing questions were already coming. First and foremost was, "Should I be questioning my own assumption about the power of answers?" I was beginning to suspect I might miss something important if I didn't listen carefully to Joseph. The notion that Grace might agree with him was also playing at the back of my mind. Was I doing too much *telling* and not enough *asking* with *her*? I suspect I already knew the answer to that question.

"Judging by the look on your face, I'm guessing you're a little unsettled right now," Joseph said. "But I assure you that once you understand how to use the Question Thinking system, particularly in strengthening your ability to observe yourself, all the pieces will fall into place. Think of this workbook as a map that will guide you into this world of questions. You have no idea what a powerful difference this can make for your career." Then he gave me an enigmatic smile and added, "To say nothing of what it can do for your personal relationships."

Question Thinking! This was going to be a challenge. Even Joseph's terms for his theories got to me. Wasn't it bad enough that he wanted me to ask myself and other people more questions? I felt like putting my hands over my ears. Was my resistance getting in the way of listening objectively to what he had to offer? No matter. I realized it was time to bite the bullet. I had to try what he had to offer. What choice did I have? I was desperate.

"This system of new tools and processes will make you more efficient, productive, and successful," Joseph continued, "and I think you'll agree there's nothing more practical than that. In the end, I believe you'll be able to make a quantum leap out of your present quandary. Despite your doubts, I'm with Alexa on this one. I'm betting on your success."

At this point Joseph declared an intermission, as he jokingly called it. I made a quick call back to my office. There was nothing that couldn't wait, which was a relief. I was feeling pretty shaken up.

I decided that when I left Joseph's office I would go to a quiet coffee shop, skim his workbook and think about my next moves. Did Joseph understand my strengths as an answer man? Was I missing something? Was *he*?

Minutes later, standing in the mirrored elevator, I looked up to catch my reflection. Staring back at me was the face of a stranger, me — filled with tension and frustration. Was this the face that Grace had been looking at for the past few months? Truth be told, I wasn't sure I'd want to hang around that guy myself. Could I really change, as Alexa and Joseph seemed to believe? And did I really want to? Maybe I should accept my strengths as a guy who's an expert on answers. Maybe I really wasn't leadership material.

3   _The Choice Map_

When we resumed this conversation, Joseph pointed to a mural on the wall of his office. I'd noticed it before but hadn't paid much attention to it. "This is what I call the Choice Map," he explained. "It helps us become better observers of the two basic paths we take in life — the Learner Path and the Judger Path. When things aren't working, you can use this map to figure out what's in your way and find a better path for getting what you want.

"Notice the figure standing at the crossroads between the two paths at the left side of the Choice Map," Joseph continued. "That represents you and me — every one of us. In every instant of our lives we're faced with choosing between the Learner Path and the Judger Path. The smaller figures show what kinds of questions we ask on each path and what happens, depending on which path we take."

From his chair Joseph directed a laser pointer at the map, swinging it back and forth between two little signs. The one by the Learner Path said, "Choose," the one by the Judger Path said, "React." I could see how imagining myself on one path or the other could be a way of observing my own choices and actions.

I followed Joseph's laser pointer to the upper path, where figures were happily jogging along. This was the Learner Path, with the sign indicating you get to it by *choosing*. It looked pretty inviting to me.

The other path, the Judger Path, looked downright bleak. It had to do with *reacting* rather than choosing. No happy joggers here. Those figures looked troubled as they headed down toward the billboard labeled *Judger*. A smaller sign warned: *Judger Pit*. The warning had obviously come too late for one fellow who was sinking in the mud. I chuckled, but my amusement ended abruptly when some unpleasant thoughts raced through my mind: *Was Joseph trying to tell me something? Did he think I was sinking in the mud like that poor guy? Did he think I was a Judger and a loser?*

"What are you thinking?" Joseph asked.

I was too nonplussed to bother trying to cover it up. "Are you implying I'm a Judger?" I looked past him, pretending to study the map. "Or that I'm a loser?"

Joseph answered quickly. "You wouldn't be in this office if anybody believed you were a loser. As for your concern about being a Judger, let me answer you this way: Every single one of us has Judger moments, including me. It's a natural part of being human."

"That makes me feel a little better," I ventured, though still ill at ease.

"Let's be clear about this," Joseph continued. "The Choice Map is about helping you observe yourself and others better. It's not about labeling people or putting them in boxes. It's a powerful guide for charting more effective paths through our lives. It illustrates what happens when we follow one of those two paths, Learner or Judger. Its message is so universal that I had this mural painted on my wall. Nobody who visits my office escapes the Choice Map." He spread out his arms expansively. "How could they miss its message?"

"I almost did," I confessed.

We both laughed and I relaxed a little.

"At nearly every moment of our lives, we're faced with choosing between taking the Learner and Judger Paths," Joseph continued. "Whether we recognize it or not, we're actually making that choice moment by moment by moment. As you can see, the Learner Path takes you to a very different place than the Judger Path. With Judger mindset we eventually end up stuck in the mud. With Learner mindset we can discover new possibilities.

The Art of the Question, Copyright ©1998 by Marilee Goldberg, Ph.D.
This material is by permission of John Wiley & Sons, Inc.

What's possible?
What are my choices?
What's best to do now?
LEARNER
Thoughtful Choices
Solution Focused
Win-Win Relating
What are they thinking, feeling, and wanting?
What am I responsible for?
Whose fault is it?
SWITCH
Ask Learner Questions to Avoid Judger Pit
Switching Lane
What's wrong with *me*?
What's wrong with *them*?
JUDGER
Automatic Reactions
Blame Focused
Win-Lose Relating
Copyright © 2009 Marilee Adams, Ph.D. *Change Your Questions, Change Your Life.*

"Most of the time, we're shifting back and forth between our Learner and Judger mindsets, barely aware we have any control over which one we've chosen. But we do have choice in every moment. Real choice begins when we can be mindful enough to observe our own thoughts and feelings and the language we use to express them. This is the key to success — the observer self! It's as simple as asking ourselves, *Where am I right now? What's present? Am I in Judger or Learner?* After all, if we can't observe our own thinking, how can we manage it, and if we can't manage our own thinking, how can we truly manage anything else?

"How about if we put it to the test right now? We've got a tailor-made issue to work with, too. Are you willing to look at what just happened when you asked if I thought you were a loser and a Judger?"

I nodded uneasily.

"Place yourself at the crossroads," Joseph said, flashing his laser pointer around the figure standing between the Learner and Judger Paths. "Something just happened to that guy. Notice the words *Thoughts, Feelings, Circumstances* near his head.

"Those words represent anything that impacts us at any moment. Some of the things that happen in life will be unpleasant: You get an unexpected bill or a phone call with terrible news. Maybe your spouse announces that a truck just backed into your new car in the parking lot. Those kinds of things can be extremely upsetting. The whole world begins to look like that mud pit at the end of the map. Stuff like that happens all the time, wouldn't you agree?"

I rolled my eyes and thought, *he doesn't know the half of it!*

"But positive events impact us, too," Joseph continued. "You click on the TV and the reporter announces that your favorite team had an unexpected win. Your boss surprises you with a fabulous job offer, or maybe your spouse sends flowers with an invitation to spend a romantic evening together. You can never tell what life will throw at you."

"I could stand more of the good stuff!" I said. "But what's the point here?"

"It comes down to this," Joseph said. "Things happen to us all the time. You don't have much choice about that. But where we do have choice is in *what we do with what happens.*"

"I like that," I said, thinking he should have that statement on the back of his business card instead of that big question mark.

"Case in point," Joseph continued, "let's examine the exact moment when I first showed you the Choice Map. Something happened that put you on the Judger Path. What do *you* think happened?"

"I don't know," I said. "I just started...I just... Something hit me and off I went."

"What kinds of questions did you ask yourself when you looked at the Choice Map?"

Damn! He'd hit the target dead center. I flushed, suddenly remembering my questions: *Does he think I'm a Judger? Does he think I'm a loser? Does he think I'm sinking in the mud? Does he think I'm hopeless?* When I looked at that map, my gut had knotted up and all these loser questions flooded my brain.

"Yeah, I admit it," I said. "I screwed up."

"Whoa!" Joseph exclaimed, holding up his hand. "There's no good or bad, no right or wrong here. There's just what happens and what you do with what happens. In those first instants, you actually made a choice to bombard yourself with negative Self-Questions."

"Like, *am I hopeless?*" I said, trying to crack a feeble smile.

"Right, and that's a good example of the kind of negative Self-Questions, or Self-Q's as I like to call them, that send us right into the Judger Pit."

"So how do I get out?" I asked.

"You observe and then choose."

"Choose?" I said incredulously.

"There's the *Judger* way and the *Learner* way. The secret of being really effective and satisfied in our lives begins with our ability to distinguish between the two —"

"So that's where choice comes in," I said, half questioning.

"Yes! That's the essence of Question Thinking," Joseph said. "Change your questions, change your thinking.

If you change your thinking, you can change almost anything else. You step into your observer self and become neutral and open-minded. If only for a second, you become an observer watching a movie of your life. You learn to simply notice whatever moods, thoughts, and behaviors are going on, without adding any layers of interpretation or judgment. This sets the stage for change. It's very different from being so immersed in the situation that you can't imagine there could be any other possibility than the way it is."

"With engineering problems," I said, "I'm always using something like this observer self to cross-check my own figures and conclusions and confirm that I'm applying the right data. But you're saying the Choice Map gives me a way of cross-checking *myself*—as you say, observing whatever moods and thoughts might be shaping the choices I'm making so I can make a course correction."

"Exactly. Have you ever had the experience of catching yourself calling somebody by the wrong name?"

"Of course."

"It's your observer self that catches the error," Joseph explained.

"So, you're talking about a natural capacity, something that everyone already has—and the Choice Map is a tool for increasing that capacity?"

Joseph nodded emphatically. "That same observer capacity gives us a chance to focus on the bigger picture. Without that, you're on automatic pilot and reacting mindlessly. The

Choice Map is about developing ways to make intentional, conscious choices rather than just reacting and allowing ourselves to be controlled by events around us. These intentional and conscious choices, moment by moment by moment, are essential leadership qualities. Are you with me?"

"I think so," I said.

"A minute ago, when you found yourself in the Judger Pit, you weren't exactly in observer mode, were you?"

Joseph was right. If I'd been a neutral observer, I wouldn't have reacted as strongly as I did. He had said nothing to even remotely imply I was a Judger or a loser. That judgmental opinion had come from only one person — me. I had gotten in the Judger Pit all by myself!

"From the look on your face," Joseph said, "you've just recognized your own Judger, maybe for the first time. Bravo! You'll understand why I congratulated you later. First I want to tell you a story about something that happened to me just last month.

"I was in a coaching session with the superintendent of a large construction company," Joseph began. "I spent twenty long minutes listening to him complain and put down everyone he worked with. According to him, the world is filled with idiots. I was getting pretty fed up with all his judgmental chatter. I felt like kicking him out of my office. Do you get the picture?"

"You were both speeding down the Judger Path." I was glad to hear I wasn't the only one who goes Judger.

"Exactly," Joseph admitted. "The questions running through my mind were, *What did I do to deserve this guy? Who does he think he is, a gift to mankind?*"

"Those are both Judger questions."

"Right! When I realized what I was doing, I almost laughed out loud. Here I was judging this man for judging other people. I was in Judger mode as much as he was!"

Joseph obviously enjoyed telling this story on himself. "By working with the Choice Map you get pretty good at catching yourself in Judger. First, you just notice that something's not quite right. Maybe you feel tense, or upset, or just plain blocked. That gives you the clue you need to ask yourself, *Am I in Judger?* If the answer is yes, then you ask, *Is this where I want to be?* I knew that if I stayed in Judger, I really couldn't help this guy, and that's what my job was. *No one can help anyone else from a Judger place.*"

> # No one can help anyone else from a Judger place.

"Seems like a good time to cut your losses and back out," I offered.

"Not at all," Joseph replied. "That's where the observer self can be so valuable, allowing us to recognize when we're in Judger and literally switch our thinking from Judger to Learner. There's a specific kind of question that helps us do that — and appropriately I call it a *Switching question.* The one that worked for me that day was, *How else can I think about him?*

"That Switching question gave me the freedom to wonder: *What does he need?* Instead of labeling him and writing him off, that Learner question helped me be *curious* about him. The Choice Map simplifies this whole process for observing yourself, discovering more options, and choosing more wisely, even under pressure."

I gave this some serious thought. "It seems like lots of people go into Judger whenever there's any kind of conflict," I said. "I mean, both people are probably in Judger at the same time. Right? That's pretty normal, isn't it?" I was thinking about that awful moment with Grace at the airport.

"It *is* normal for Judger to reign when people are in conflict," Joseph said. "When both people are in Judger, everything comes to a screeching halt. But here's a million dollar tip for you: *When two people are in Judger, the one who wakes up first has an advantage.* That person can choose to go Learner and turn the situation around for both of them."

Something clicked for me. I'd noticed after some disagreements with Grace that she would switch from stubbornness to open-mindedness, often very quickly. Her ability to switch always lightened things up between us. I had often wondered if she did this naturally or if she had some inner trick. She once told me all she did was remember the big picture — our relationship was more important than proving she was right. I'd noticed that when Grace switched like that, I often got calmer too. If Joseph's techniques could teach me how to do this on purpose, I'd be way ahead of the game with Charles, my nemesis at work.

I was starting to fidget. "Look," I said. "What's the bottom line?"

"There's really just one lesson here — with the questions we ask ourselves, consciously or not, we literally put ourselves either in Learner or Judger mode. And we're most effective at virtually everything we do when we're in Learner.

"But don't worry if you take the Judger Path every once in a while. Being human, we always will from time to time. The real issue is whether we'll dig in our heels and stay there. That's what really causes problems. When your observer self becomes stronger and more dependable, you'll find it much easier to switch your questions and get back into Learner. That's where things open up again and you can effectively go toward the results you're looking for."

"You make it sound so easy," I said, thinking about the awful results that had landed me in Joseph's office.

"Ah, but it *is* easier than you think," Joseph said. "The signals for catching yourself in Judger are obvious once you know how to spot them. Your body and your moods will tell you. Remember what happened to me with the superintendent? I wasn't getting any place with him until I stepped into my observer self and recognized that my own mood was getting in the way.

"Later, he and I talked about moods and attitudes we associate with Judger — *self-righteousness, arrogance, superiority,* and *defensiveness* headed up the list. Add to that the habit of putting others down — or putting ourselves down — and you've got a prescription for a real mess. The questions we ask ourselves, whether conscious or not, can either be our worst enemies, or our greatest friends. I've discovered that any time I get into negative moods, Judger questions and attitudes are involved. Realizing that, I can change my questions and turn things around, sometimes very quickly, for a very different result."

"So you're saying my body tells me what my mind is doing? It even indicates the kinds of questions I'm asking myself?"

"In fact, yes," Joseph said. "You're a researcher. Let's do an experiment. I'm going to recite two different sets of questions. All you need to do is notice how each set of questions impacts you. Pay attention to your muscles, your posture, your breathing, and what you're feeling in different areas of your body."

He got up, walked over to the Choice Map, and stood in front of the Judger Pit. "Ask yourself these questions:

Whose fault is it?
What's wrong with me?

Why am I such a failure?
Why is everybody so stupid and frustrating?
Haven't we already been there, done that?
Why bother?"

As he recited these questions, my chest tightened up. My shoulders stiffened. I was clutching up like a rookie pitcher in the last minutes of an important game. I laughed uncomfortably, "I think I see what you mean. I definitely feel some tension here and there."

"I thought you might. Almost everyone I've done this experiment with has some kind of reaction. What are some words you'd use to describe how those questions made you feel?"

I shrugged. "Just slightly uncomfortable, I guess."

"How about something a little more specific?"

I could see that Joseph wasn't going to let me off the hook. He was really pushing me. I decided to be honest with him, though it wasn't easy admitting even to myself what I was feeling.

"Well," I began, "I feel like that guy in the Judger Pit, stuck, bogged down." I was stumbling around with this. I wasn't used to putting words to my feelings.

"I know this isn't easy," Joseph said. "People in my workshops come up with a variety of words: Hopeless and helpless. Pessimistic. Negative. Depleted. Depressed. Uptight. Victim. Loser."

Learner/Judger Questions

Judger
What's wrong?
Whose fault is it?
What's wrong with me?
How can I prove I'm right?
How will this be a problem?
Why is that person so stupid
   and frustrating?
How can I be in control?
Why bother?

Learner
What works?
What am I responsible for?
What do I want?
What can I learn?
What are the facts? What's
   useful about this?
What is the other person
   thinking, feeling, and wanting?
What's the big picture?
What's possible?

*We all ask both kinds of questions, and we have the power to
choose which ones to ask in any moment.*

Joseph was right on! Every one of those words struck a chord with me.

"As you learn to pick up on those body clues and observe your moods and thoughts," Joseph said, "catching yourself in Judger will get quicker and easier.

"Here, let's try something. Experiment with giving yourself sixty seconds to just observe whatever is going on with you right now. Are you game?"

Intrigued, I let out a breath, imagined myself as an observer, and pretended I was watching myself sitting there in Joseph's office. I noticed my feelings beginning to shift. The changes were subtle at first. "Aha! It's like you were saying," I told him. "I am moving away from those negative feelings."

"Good. Later on, I'll give you more tools for doing that," Joseph said. "Once your observer skills are stronger, you'll be able to zero in on what kinds of questions are getting you stuck. Then you'll be able to craft new questions to carry you right into Learner territory. This way, you can have your questions, rather than your questions having you.

"All right. That's enough of Judger for now. Would you like to experience a different set of questions?"

I nodded emphatically.

"Then let's check out the Learner Path," Joseph said, as he moved to a different part of the Choice Map. I think he asked me to breathe normally and center myself for a few seconds before going on.

"Okay, good!" Joseph said. "Imagine that you're asking yourself these questions:

What happened?

What do I want?

What's useful about this?

What's the other person thinking, feeling, and wanting?

What can I learn?

What are my choices?

What's best to do now?

What's possible?"

Almost immediately I experienced a quiet excitement. My breathing got easier. I began feeling a willingness and openness I certainly hadn't felt with the first set of questions. One thing was particularly noticeable: My shoulders relaxed. I hadn't felt this good in a while!

"How's that?" Joseph asked, smiling.

"What a difference! I like it."

"What are some words you'd use to describe this second experience?"

"Open," I said. "Lighter. Upbeat. Curious. More energy. Optimistic. A little hopeful...maybe there are solutions to my problems after all."

"Good! Good," Joseph reiterated. "These feelings signal that you've taken yourself into Learner mindset."

At that moment I heaved a great sigh of relief. I might not have totally understood or even agreed with what Joseph was saying, but for the first time in a while I was feeling a little hopeful. Maybe this guy actually did have some tools that could make a difference for me, as nutty as it might seem.

You can download a free color copy of the Choice Map at:
www.InquiryInstitute.com.

4 We're All Recovering Judgers

We took a short break while Joseph went off to get us coffee in the kitchenette adjacent to his office. He was gone long enough for me to check my cell phone for messages. One of them, from Grace, was about her young assistant Jennifer, who had messed up yet another assignment. "I've just got to vent," Grace was saying. "I feel like I'm two seconds from firing her. Can you call me right back?" I snapped my phone shut. *Why was Grace bothering me at work? Couldn't she handle Jennifer by herself? Did she think I needed her problems on top of mine?* My jaw and shoulders clenched up.

Just then Joseph returned with a tray that held two full coffee mugs and containers of cream and sugar. I took a mug and some cream, glad to focus on stirring what was in my cup. I needed to settle myself down so I could listen to what Joseph was starting to tell me. He was back to his story about the superintendent.

"My client and I both had a breakthrough that day," he was saying, "right after I recognized I had gotten hijacked by Judger. After I changed my questions and switched into Learner mindset, everything was different."

"But did the guy *get* it?" I was asking myself the same question — *Did I get it?* Something about that superintendent's story was making me uneasy. But what was it?

> # With Judger mindset, the future can only be a recycled version of the past.

"Oh, sure he did," Joseph said. "In the end, he made an interesting comment. With the 'Judger agenda,' as he called it, 'the costs can be tremendous. The future can only be a recycled version of the past. And with the Learner program the power is on. The juice is flowing. You can actually make a new future for yourself.'"

Suddenly I knew what was bugging me.

"You make it sound like any kind of judgment is a bad

thing," I interrupted. "But I disagree. I could never do my job without making judgments…and I take a lot of pride in making good judgments. You have to judge when you're making technological choices, or when you're choosing a vendor to buy from, or whether you're assigning the best person to do a certain job."

"By all means," Joseph said. "You bring up an important point. Having good judgment, developing the ability to make discerning choices, is essential, especially, I would imagine, in a job like yours. But I'm not talking about judgment. I'm talking about being judgment*al*. They're not the same thing at all. It's a shame those words even sound alike. One of my dictionaries defines judgment*al* as 'attacking self or others.' Nothing could be more different from exercising good judgment."

"So Judger mindset is always judgmental," I said.

"That's right," Joseph said, taking a sip of coffee, "Judger is always judgmental. What's more, Judger has two faces—either we're being judgmental about ourselves or about other people."

I fell silent, trying to absorb what he was telling me. I'd certainly gotten judgmental when I listened to Grace's message. I'd jumped right into Judger. But Grace calling me at work about Jennifer wasn't exactly using the best judgment, either. Or was I being judgmental about that, too?

Joseph settled back into his chair. "What's going through your mind right now?" he asked.

"I can't deny that I've been spending a lot of time in Judger lately," I began hesitantly. "But how do you avoid going down that path when you've got a guy like Charles to deal with? He's the source of a lot of the problems with our team and with our miserable results. He's driving me nuts." I clamped my jaw shut, not wanting to say anything more. I didn't like thinking about myself as being so much in Judger. In fact, I was really starting to resent this Judger stuff. Besides, how do you stay on the Learner Path with problems piling up all around you?

> # We're all recovering Judgers.

Joseph must have read my mind because the next thing he said was, "It's important to remember that slipping into Judger is just part of being human, especially when things aren't going well. In this respect, we're all recovering Judgers. No doubt about it, our Judger nature can be a bit addictive. We can't ever get rid of Judger, but we *can* learn to manage it. Awareness, commitment, and courage — with a dash of humor — that's what it takes to keep bringing ourselves back to Learner.

"The whole idea is to accept Judger and practice Learner, moment by moment by moment. This work is not about getting on the Learner Path and staying there.

That's a pipe dream. Real personal power depends on how good we get at recovering from Judger once it takes over. That's why I got such a kick out of that situation with my superintendent client. Sure I got hijacked by Judger, but the instant I realized it, I could rescue myself and get back on the Learner Path. Sometimes it's even fun to see how fast I can catch Judger and how fast I can recover.

"Frankly," Joseph said with a smile, "sometimes I find myself slipping into Judger several times an hour! By the way, in your workbook you'll find a tool called *Make Friends with Judger*."

> # Accept Judger and practice Learner—moment by moment by moment.

The idea of having to deal with Judger forever didn't please me very much. On the other hand, at least it meant I wasn't any worse than anyone else.

Joseph paused for a moment, then said, "Tell me about Charles."

"He's second in command on the project team I head up," I said, hoping my exasperation didn't show too much. "But this guy challenges everything I say. I must admit, he's probably got a legitimate bone to pick with me. He was passed over for the position I got, and boy, does he resent it.

I would, too, if I were in his shoes! He's a real know-it-all, picky and petty. He's out to sabotage me. That's the bottom line. And it looks like he's succeeding."

"When you think about Charles, what's the first question that pops into your mind?"

I chuckled. "That's easy! *How can I put a leash on this guy before he destroys me?*"

"Anything else?"

"Lots of things! *How can I stay in control? Aren't I supposed to be the one who's the leader of this team? How can I make this guy get with the program?*"

"And?"

"*How did I ever get myself into this mess? Whatever made me think I could handle being a leader?*" I paused for a moment, then asserted, "Listen, the thing is, Charles needs to change as much as you think I do."

> # Change begins with the person who wants the change.

"That may be true," Joseph said. "But you're the one in my office now. Change begins with the person who wants the change. Right?"

That really knocked the wind out of my sails. I sat back in my chair and took a deep breath. "What am I supposed to do, ignore the fact that he stabs me in the back

58

Chapter 4

every chance he gets?" I was getting steamed. "There's no way to separate my reactions from what Charles does!"

"Ah, but that's the beauty of it," Joseph said. "You *can* separate your reactions from his behavior — and anyone else's. Until you do, you'll keep giving away your power. You'll be just like a puppet, with no control of your own. Anybody, including Charles, will be able to pull your strings. It's a matter of whether you have your Judger or your Judger has you."

> # Either you have your Judger
> # or your Judger has you.

"I'm not agreeing or disagreeing with you," I said, secretly seething inside. "I don't think I could possibly see this situation with Charles differently."

"Is that a question?" Joseph asked.

"What are you saying?"

"Can you reshape that statement as a question?"

"You mean, like, *How else can I think about this?*" To my surprise, the moment I asked myself this question I felt a subtle shift inside me. For one thing, I let go of the breath I hadn't known I was holding, and my shoulders relaxed enough that Joseph probably noticed too.

"Exactly. Did you notice? You just switched yourself into Learner. Quick as that. And here's my answer: No matter what Charles or anyone else might do, you can use the Choice Map, and what you're learning about your body's messages, to identify when you've gone into Judger. Those messages will remind you to stand back and observe where you are. You will have empowered your observer self, so you can watch your own movie for a moment. Then you'll be able to tell the difference between what Charles does and *what you choose to do with what he does.*"

I tried to take in Joseph's lesson. It wasn't easy. Judger questions were still running through my brain. I guess Judger had a grip on me where Charles was concerned, not to mention in my marriage.

"Go back for a moment to that person standing at the crossroads," Joseph said, pointing at the Choice Map. "Remember, that figure represents every one of us at any moment when we're hit with something and we have to deal with it. We're stumped. Regardless of the situation, it's vital to remember we have choice about how to respond to it. Do you know what those choices are?"

"We can just react and jump right into Judger," I said, feeling my way along. "Or we can pause, check in with our moods and body feelings and notice what kinds of Self-Q's we're asking, then try to choose Learner. We can choose…we have choices."

Fireworks started going off in my mind. *I actually do have choice! And I can choose Learner when I want to.* Maybe Joseph's tools really could make a difference with my results at work.

"I have to say," I told him cautiously, "maybe it's not as difficult to distinguish between Judger and Learner as I thought."

Joseph actually applauded. "Yes. Yes, that's great! Once you're able to observe your own thinking, and recognize the differences between Learner and Judger, you grab hold of the power of choice." Joseph seemed tremendously excited by this notion. "You're a quick study," he exclaimed. "I see another of the traits Alexa values in you so much." He glanced at his wristwatch. "It's a little after one o'clock now. Let's stop here for the day."

Joseph opened a drawer in his desk and took out some copies of the Choice Map.

"Take these with you," he said, handing them to me. "Study the Choice Map when you get to your office. And take one home to post on your refrigerator."

I groaned inwardly. What on earth would I tell Grace about all this! She'd want to know where I'd gotten the Choice Map and why I'd put it on the refrigerator.

"This map illustrates fundamental distinctions between Learner and Judger mindsets," Joseph said, as we walked down the hall. "Ultimately, the message is pretty simple. *Change your questions, change your results.* This is core self-management know-how for every recovering Judger."

> ## Change your questions, change your results.

At the doors of his outer office, Joseph stopped and turned to face me. Over his shoulder, on the wall with the Question Thinking Hall of Fame, I spotted a picture of Alexa. It appeared to be from a major magazine, profiling her for some award. Embarrassed though I was to admit it, I hadn't known about this article. Given how long I'd known Alexa I certainly should have.

"See you next time," Joseph said, shaking my hand warmly.

My head was spinning. My whole life was being turned upside down. What really puzzled me was that I also felt lighter, more optimistic than I'd been in ages. One thing Alexa was right about — this Joseph guy had a provocative way of looking at how to make changes in our lives. I began to imagine that maybe, by working with him, I'd come up with answers — or was it new questions — that could put my career back on track.

5   *Kitchen Talk*

It was early in the morning when Grace found the Choice Map I had stuck on the refrigerator door the night before. As usual, I awoke to the smell of fresh coffee and made my way downstairs to the kitchen. Grace is always up before me. She's one of those people who wakes up cheerful and enthusiastic about each new day. I'm just the opposite and I know it sometimes puts Grace on edge. She claims that I'm like a bear coming out of hibernation in the morning. I don't think I'm quite that bad, but I don't exactly start the day off with a song in my heart.

As I entered the kitchen, I found Grace standing in

front of the refrigerator with her back to me. She appeared to be engrossed with the Choice Map. I was immediately worried about what she might say. I was pretty sure she'd start probing and I'd have to tell her the whole thing — about my trouble at work and all the rest of it. That would lead to how I'd gotten the Choice Map and why I'd posted it on the refrigerator. Then I might have to tell her about why Alexa had referred me to Joseph and that could turn into an emotional minefield.

While I was worrying about how I would avoid telling her the whole story, Grace suddenly turned around and gave me a big hug.

"Where did you get this?" she asked. "It's terrific!"

She took the Choice Map off the refrigerator door and started waving it around in her hand. I mumbled something about it being a handout for a special training at work and then poured a cup of coffee for myself and one for Grace.

"I'm amazed," she said. "I've already learned something from this. You remember that message I left you about Jennifer, my assistant at work? I guess I've been riding her pretty hard lately. I can just feel her cringing any time I get within a few feet of her. Looking at the Choice Map, I realize I've been a real Judger with her, like it says here, and I'm sure that's put her on edge. She's been messing up a lot, but this makes me wonder if I've been contributing to the problem. After all, nobody does their best work when their boss is expecting the worst from them."

"It's all in the kinds of questions you ask." I didn't even think before the words just popped out of my mouth.

"What questions?" Grace asked. "I don't ever get that far with poor Jennifer."

"According to this guy Joseph, who gave me this map..."

"Wait," Grace interrupted. "Who's Joseph?"

I stared at her blankly for a moment, debating about whether to tell her the truth. I decided to keep things simple. "He's this consultant Alexa hired," I told her, determined not to go into any more details than absolutely necessary. Yesterday, right after meeting with Joseph, I'd spent an hour studying the map, preparing answers for any questions Grace might have. "He claims that most of the time we're not even aware of the questions we ask ourselves or other people. That's what the Choice Map teaches. It's a reminder to look carefully at those questions because they affect how we think and act, and how other people respond to us."

Grace looked puzzled. I pressed close to her and pointed to the little guy at the crossroads. "There's the key right there," I said, pointing to the words *Thoughts, Feelings, Circumstances* near the figure's head. "The moment anything happens to us, that's when we start asking ourselves questions. The sooner we recognize what we're asking, the better. That way we have more options." *Was this really me talking?* I was amazed at how much I recalled of Joseph's teachings. The more we talked, the more comfortable I was getting with this QT stuff.

"The main thing I see are these two paths," Grace said, tracing first one and then the other with her finger. "Take the Learner route and you'll move right along. See. This guy is saying, 'What do I want? What are my choices?' This other one is asking, 'What can I learn?' Oh, you're right, these are all questions. And the guy on the Judger Path, he's all caught up with different questions like, 'Whose fault is it? What's wrong with them?' I'll tell you, Ben, at the office, every time I hear a pin drop or somebody sigh, the first thing that pops into my head is, 'Oh, Lord, what's wrong now? What else can Jennifer possibly mess up?' And then, in a flash, I'm down on her. Do you know what she did yesterday, Ben? She...oh, hold it. That's taking me right into Judger territory, isn't it?"

"The way it works," I explained, "is that from moment to moment, stuff happens. Good stuff and bad stuff. It sort of hits us unawares. Then, especially if we have a strong Judger habit, our questions tend to follow that same pattern. If we're more in Learner, we'll ask questions in that direction."

"Action follows thought," Grace added. "It's a basic principle. But I never thought about it in terms of questions. *Action follows questions.* Seems to me the trick is just to keep ourselves in a Learner frame of mind."

"According to Joseph," I told Grace, "it's natural to slip

into Judger now and then. In fact, we alternate between the two mindsets all the time. It's just human nature." Even as I said those words, I was thinking about the argument she and I got into that day I dropped her off at the airport. I was still feeling embarrassed about how I'd treated her. I wasn't ready to go into all that with Grace, but at least I summoned up the nerve to mention part of it.

"It's so easy to go into Judger," I said, carefully choosing my words. "For example, the other day I was trying to pull out into traffic and nearly got hit by a taxi that was going about twice the speed it should have. I instantly went into Judger. It was like a bolt of lightning, you know? It happened that fast. In an instant, I was ready to punch the guy out."

"Sometimes you really worry me," Grace said, shaking her head.

My shoulders tensed up and I was on the verge of defending myself. I knew she didn't approve of my driving habits, though I'd never had an accident. We'd gotten into arguments about this, but this time a part of me stopped and said, *Don't go there, buddy.* I took a deep breath, shrugged my shoulders, and just tried to keep things easy and relaxed.

"It's just an example. What I now see, thanks to Joseph's Choice Map, is how that close call immediately put me in Judger. I was angry as hell for the next couple of hours. It was a *Judger highjack*."

I really wanted to tell Grace the whole story, about

how I'd lumped together everything I'd been experiencing lately. I'd been stewing about whether or not to resign. I was irritated about having to meet with Joseph. I was hurt, worried about my whole career going up in smoke, and angry with Grace for pressuring me about our relationship in the midst of all this. My life had become just one big...well, one big Judger Pit, I guess, and I had been sinking in the mud.

I tensed all over as I realized I'd been as much of a challenge to Joseph as that judgmental superintendent he'd told me about. That first day I'd slouched into his office, certain that meeting with him was a hopeless waste of my time. In the mood I'd been in, it was a miracle anything he said had gotten through to me. Now I was telling Grace about Joseph's ideas as if I actually knew what I was talking about!

"I'm thinking this map is a good reminder of what happens to me when I get stuck in one of my Judger-heads," Grace said. She turned away for a moment and sat down at the breakfast table. She sipped her coffee and nibbled toast as she studied the map before her. I continued standing, leaning against the counter, watching her. After a moment, Grace looked up a little shyly.

"Maybe this could help us...you know, in our relationship," she said. "What do you think?" There was not the slightest hint of blame or judgment in her voice. I was really grateful for that.

"Joseph says that life is filled with those moments

when something hits us and sets us off on one path or another...."

"But what do *you* think," Grace asked, "I mean, about it helping us — you and me?"

This time I thought I detected a bit of an edge in her voice. She really wanted me to tell her exactly what I was thinking. "As I said," I answered. "I think it applies well to any and all areas of our lives. We can all use better tools."

"What's that supposed to mean, better tools?" she asked, sounding definitely irritated.

I tried to ignore Grace's eyes. So far our conversation had gone so well, I didn't want it to turn sour. I was already asking myself, *What stupid thing did I say to mess things up again? And why did she bring up our relationship in the first place? Talk about bad timing!* And then I caught myself. Those simple little questions were pushing me right down the Judger Path. This time, though, I saw it coming. I imagined Joseph as a coach on the sidelines shouting to me, *Learner! Learner! Remember the Choice Map! Change your questions! You can turn this around!* Almost instantly a new question occurred to me: *How can I keep things positive between us?*

"Sorry," Grace was saying. "I just realized I was starting to go Judger on you."

For a moment I felt puzzled, then relieved as it dawned on me what had happened. Grace had started going down the Judger Path. We both had. And then she stopped herself, and so did I. *Amazing!* In spite of myself, I smiled.

"What are you smiling about?" Grace asked. She got up from the table, took her dishes to the sink, then turned to face me.

"Sweetheart," I said. "You're wonderful!" I took her in my arms and held her close. She stiffened but quickly softened and hugged me back.

"Do you remember that night when we had dinner at the Metropol and I was late?" I asked. I felt her nod her head against my shoulder.

"We really got into it, didn't we, about who got their times mixed up. Then you did a remarkable thing. You suddenly just dropped the whole argument and everything shifted. We got connected again. Do you remember?"

"Mm hmm, I sure do!" She chuckled, planting a kiss on my cheek.

It was difficult being serious while remembering that night, but I really wanted to get my point across. "Joseph talks about switching from Judger to Learner, and how we can do that with a single question."

"Like when I ask myself, *Do I want to win this argument? Or, do I want to have a good time?*" Grace drew away from me but kept her hands on my shoulders.

"Is that how you do your magic?" I asked.

"Some of it," she said, leaning into me again. "But I never thought of it in terms of questions."

"I'm serious," I said, wanting to make certain I got my point across. "I just realized that you're a natural at the very thing Joseph teaches. I'll bet you do it by changing your questions, even if you're not aware of it. You take yourself straight to Learner. That's how you shift your mood."

"I like those shifts!"

"Me, too," I said, hugging her again. I still wanted to know more about how she made those shifts. "How did you learn to do that?"

Before she could answer, the electronic timer chirped on the stove. Grace always sets it to alert her when it's time to get ready for work.

"Oh, no!" She sighed, suddenly all businesslike. "I'm sorry, Ben. I'd love to call in late but I really can't. I have an important meeting this morning."

In the next instant, she was dashing up the stairs to finish getting ready. Twenty minutes later she kissed me goodbye and raced out the door. When I got around to pouring myself another cup of coffee, I glanced at the refrigerator and realized the Choice Map was gone. Grace had taken it to work with her!

As I was getting in my car to leave for the office, I noticed a piece of paper stuck under the windshield wiper. It was a hurriedly written note from Grace:

Darling,

Thank you so much for the Choice Map — and especially for the good talk this morning. You can't imagine how much it meant to me!

Love, Grace

I'd never expected Grace to take the Choice Map. I felt great about the note. Clearly she liked Joseph's ideas. At least for now, I'd redeemed myself in her eyes. Good! That was one less pressure in my life.

6   *Switching Questions*

As I stepped off the elevator at the Pearl Building, I found Joseph watering his ficus trees with a large red watering can. It surprised me to see him doing something I would have handed off to my staff. He turned to me with a friendly smile. "I love having plants around. It's a daily reminder that all living things require our attention," he said. "No office should be without at least a plant or two. My wife, Sarah, is the gardener in our family. She says plants force you to ask questions. Are they getting enough water, enough sun? Do they need a little pruning? Do they need special nutrients? They thrive on questions, just like humans do." He quickly finished his gardening chores and we went inside.

"When we finished our last meeting, we were talking about the Choice Map and what it tells us about Learner and Judger mindsets," Joseph began. "Have you had any further thoughts about any of this?"

I guardedly told him about Grace, our talk in the kitchen, and how she'd taken the Choice Map from the refrigerator to work with her.

"It's clear that we get different results depending on which of the two paths we take — Learner or Judger," I told Joseph hesitantly. "Maybe I get stuck in Judger more than I'd like to admit."

"Fortunately, there's a fast track out of Judger. Look at this lane in the middle." Joseph pointed to the little road joining the Judger and Learner Paths. A sign labeled it the *Switching Lane*. "That lane is the key to change. You get to Learner by asking Switching questions. Let's look at how that works.

"When you're standing in Judger," Joseph continued, "the whole world can look pretty bleak. Even though the world is filled with infinite possibilities, we have only limited access to noticing them when seeing with Judger eyes or hearing with Judger ears. Let me show you how to change your viewpoint, how to literally see and hear differently, sometimes almost immediately. For a moment, locate yourself on the Judger Path, right where the Switching Lane begins."

I turned my attention to the map and found the Switching Lane.

"Any time you step onto this path," he continued, pointing to the Switching Lane, "you automatically step into choice. You wake up. You unveil a whole new view of the world. You literally switch how you're thinking about what's possible. When you observe your own thoughts, especially Judger ones, you gain the ability to choose freely what to think and do next."

"You're talking about choice like it's something we possess...a capacity."

"Absolutely! We're all born with that capacity," Joseph exclaimed. "That's what makes us human. Choice is always ours, although it takes practice, and sometimes courage, to make the best use of it. The author Viktor Frankl spoke of

'…the last of human freedoms — to choose one's attitude in any given circumstances, to choose one's own way.'

"And making this practical is what it's all about. That's where the rubber hits the road. Whenever you sense you might be in Judger, pause, take a deep breath, get curious, and ask yourself, *Am I in Judger?* If the answer is yes, you can step onto the Switching Lane by asking simple questions like: *Do I want to be in Judger?* and *Where would I like to be?*" Joseph laughed. "Is it easy? Not always, but it *is* simple. The Switching Lane takes you quickly to the Learner Path. You'll find a list of Switching questions in your workbook. That list is another of the tools in the QT system."

Something was nagging at the back of my mind, but I couldn't quite get hold of it. Then it dawned on me. I remembered asking Grace how she shifted her moods so quickly. I realized she used Switching questions, whether she was aware of it or not.

Joseph was gazing thoughtfully out the window. "Let me tell you a story that illustrates how Switching questions can make a huge difference in performance and results. It's a true story about my daughter Kelly, who's an avid gymnast. In college, she was even training for a national championship competition.

"Here's what happened. During training Kelly would perform quite well most of the time, but only *most* of the time. Sarah and I knew she'd never make the team that way. Her performance was too erratic.

"So, upon her request, we worked with Kelly so she could make the improvement she needed to make the team. First, we asked her what she thought about just before a performance. She discovered that in those crucial moments she always asked just one basic question, *Will I fall this time?*"

"Which is a Judger question," I observed.

"Right," Joseph said. "And asking it led to what my daughter calls *Judger trouble*. That question really interfered with her performance. So the three of us worked on finding a Switching question she could ask herself instead to propel her quickly into Learner. The new question was Kelly's own idea: *How can I do a great job?* That did the trick. Using that new question, she reprogrammed herself by directing her attention in a positive direction. Her performance improved exponentially and also became highly predictable. Kelly says that new question helps her stay in *the zone*."

"Did she make the team?"

"She sure did," Joseph said. "And by the way, she came home with a trophy. It wasn't first place but I was really proud. I have to confess that 20 years ago, I would have probably chastised her for not taking first place. Oh, I tell you, having children teaches us to ask a whole new set of questions! By the way, you'll find Kelly's story in my Question Thinking Hall of Fame."

"This all sounds like a bit of magic, to me," I quipped. "Or a miracle."

"It's neither magic nor a miracle," Joseph replied,

smiling. "It's a *method*. With questions we can even change ourselves physiologically. For example, the question *What if I get fired?* can set off a whole chain of biochemical stress reactions in your body. Kelly's question, *Will I fall this time?* made her anxious, which interfered with her performance and reinforced any old programming for failure. Consciously, of course, she didn't want to fail, but it's exactly what happened anyway with that old question. *Thought sets intention.* Learner questions program us with a positive intention — in Kelly's case, for the right attitude and moves for an outstanding performance."

"By implication you're suggesting that Judgers can't be top performers," I reflected. "I can't agree with you there. I've known Judger types who produced quite a lot."

"Be careful about using labels like 'Judger types.' There isn't anybody who's a Judger person or a Learner person. These terms refer only to *mindsets* and, as you know by now, every one of us has *both* mindsets and always will. That's the conundrum of being human. The problem with labels is that they can become permanent, and that makes changing seem impossible. On the other hand, our mindsets are *dynamic*; they can change from minute to minute. The point is that Question Thinking puts us more in charge of making the changes we want.

"But you are absolutely right that many people spend more time in Judger than Learner," Joseph said. "And they may be quite driven and productive. However, their success often comes with very high costs. People with an overactive Judger can drive themselves and everyone around them nuts, and that lowers productivity, cooperation, and creativity. It's hard to feel loyal to or trust someone who has a high Judger quotient. Operating from Judger can build resentment and conflict, whether with your family or your co-workers.

"If you want people to be really engaged and involved, Learner is the path to take. An organization led by people in high Judger tends to have greater levels of stress, conflict, and people problems. Those kinds of leaders are not well equipped to be flexible and adaptable — or successful — in meeting challenges. And just imagine the havoc that Judger plays when you take that mindset home with you at night!

"My wife, Sarah, once wrote an article exploring the difference between Judger marriages and Learner marriages. Her premise was that our experience of intimate relationships will be very different depending on whether we look on our partner with Learner eyes or Judger eyes. Sarah points out that with Learner eyes we're able to focus on what we appreciate about the other person and what's working in our relationship, at least most of the time. We build from strengths rather than dwelling on flaws — our own or our partner's."

I nodded, thinking that this made sense.

"When we're in Judger, whether at home or work, everything can seem like a roadblock. When that happens we need to go back to basic Switching questions, like: *Am I in Judger? Will it get me what I really want? Where would I rather be?* Pause, take a deep breath, put yourself on the Switching Lane and you can step right onto the Learner Path."

"If what you say is true, I could just stay in Learner by always keeping those questions in mind."

"Theoretically, yes. But life really isn't that simple. And not one of us is a saint. We're all going to fall into Judger from time to time — that's the point I'm emphasizing when I say we're all *recovering Judgers*," Joseph continued. "But I promise you this — the more you take to heart the Choice Map and Switching questions, the faster you'll be able to step into Learner, the easier it will be, and the longer you'll be able to stay there. You'll also spend less time in Judger and the experience itself is usually less intense, so the consequences of being there will be minimized.

"And remember," Joseph continued, "Judger has two faces, one being judgmental toward *ourselves*, the other being judgmental toward *others*. The results can look quite different but they come from that same judgmental place.

"If we focus our Judger mindset on ourselves, for example, with questions such as, *Why am I such a failure?* we hurt our self-confidence and may even feel depressed. On the other hand, if we focus our Judger mindset on others, with questions such as, *Why is everyone around me so stupid and frustrating?* we tend to get angry, resentful, and hostile. Either way, with Judger, we end up in some kind of conflict either with ourselves or with others. When Judger takes control it's impossible to find genuine resolution or any sense of peace. That's why lots of mediators also use the Learner/Judger material, especially the Choice Map.

"Let me give you an example of Judger when we aim it at ourselves. Years ago, Sarah was talking with Ruth, her editor at one of the magazines she writes for. They were sharing how they had both had issues with their weight. Sarah told Ruth how she used the Choice Map to help her make better choices about eating. Ruth got so excited, she asked Sarah to write an article about her experiences.

"In the article, Sarah described how the questions people typically ask themselves about eating either get them in trouble with their weight or help them be successful and content about it. The troublemaker questions she listed included, *What's wrong with me? Why am I out of control again? Why am I such a bad person?*"

"Those are all judgmental questions," I interjected.

"Right. And whenever Sarah started down the Judger Path with questions like those, she really beat herself up, which of course sent her spiraling right down to the Judger Pit. Unfortunately, those Judger meltdowns usually caused her to feel out of control and eat even more. Sometimes that led to real bingeing. Once Sarah recognized the impact those troublemaker Judger questions had on her, she decided to look for Switching questions to rescue herself. She said that

Switching questions are the best thing she's ever found for getting back in control. Her new questions included: *Am I willing to forgive myself?* and, *How do I want to feel?*"

"Which got her onto the Switching Lane, her shortcut back to Learner," I said.

"Right again. Once she switched into Learner, she figured out some questions to help her stay there: *What will serve me best right now? Am I being honest with myself? What can I do to feel better that doesn't involve eating?* Whenever she asked herself one of these questions she felt empowered rather than out of control. Not only that, she's gotten herself in great shape. She tells me it's pretty easy to maintain now."

Judging by the photos of Sarah on Joseph's desk, she certainly didn't look like a woman with weight issues. But all this talk was making me even more uncomfortably aware of how often the questions I asked myself were straight out of a Judger mindset.

"From what I've seen so far," Joseph said, in a surprisingly accepting tone of voice, "while you obviously don't have trouble with your weight, you still have a lot of self-Judger going on."

"I can't disagree," I hedged. "But what's your basis for saying that?"

"That's easy," Joseph said. "Do you remember that time you were so sure I saw you as a Judger *and* a loser?"

"Yes," I said, hesitantly, sensing I was stepping into something I would regret.

"That's the perspective that keeps you bogged down and resigned about being able to change. But while you aim judgmental questions at yourself," Joseph said, looking straight at me, "you're also pretty good at targeting other people."

"I agree I can be pretty hard on myself…and on other people." I began to squirm. "But sometimes people really are jerks and idiots. I know I'm right about that. You've got to accept this as a fact of life and exercise good common sense, or good judgment, as you already said."

Without comment, Joseph directed my attention back to the Choice Map. As I held it in my hand, he leaned forward and pointed at the figure that was starting down the Judger Path. Then he pointed to the thought bubble over his head. It contained just one question, which I read out loud, "Whose fault is it?"

What jumped into my mind were all the troubles I'd been having at work. I focused on that stark moment of truth when I concluded I was a failure and would have to resign. The shame I felt was just awful. Did Judger have a hand in shame, too? I was certainly in my Judger-head at that moment, having judged myself as a loser. But wasn't I justified? I couldn't deny I'd screwed up.

"What's going through your mind right now?"

I replied with discomfort, "The more we talk, the more I see I've got to accept the blame for a lot of what's happened."

"Blame," Joseph said. "Tell me exactly what that word means to you."

"The bottom line? It means I should step down. I'm the incompetent one here. Period! End of conversation."

"Back up for a moment. Change your question from 'Who's to *blame*' to 'What am I *responsible* for?'"

I thought about this for a moment. "Blame. Responsibility. Aren't they the same thing?"

"Not at all," Joseph said. "Blame is Judger. Responsibility is Learner. There's a world of difference between them. Focusing on blame blinds us from seeing real alternatives and solutions. It's almost impossible to fix a problem when operating from blame. Blame can be paralyzing. Blame keeps us stuck in the past. Responsibility, on the other hand, paves the path for a better future. If you focus your questions on what you might be responsible for, you also open your mind to new possibilities. You're free to create alternatives that lead to positive change."

> # Blame keeps us stuck in the past. Responsibility paves the path for a better future.

"Paralyzing?" What did he mean by that? I felt an urge to get up, stretch, and walk around. I took a break, went to the bathroom, splashed some cold water on my face. After

I returned, Joseph said, "Remind me what you said about Charles the other day."

Ah, back to Charles! Now I knew I was on solid ground. It would be easy to prove to Joseph how good judgment served me in this case, that my feelings about Charles were not just the product of Judger attitudes. "I told you, if it weren't for Charles I wouldn't be in this mess," I said. "That's obvious. He's playing a win-lose game. You'd have to be blind not to see that."

Without replying, Joseph directed me to turn to my workbook and find the pages labeled *Learner/Judger Chart: Mindsets and Relationships.* I studied it for a moment, checking out the two columns that listed key characteristics of Learner and Judger. The content of those two columns was very different. It hit me immediately how one way of thinking would take me down the Judger Path while the other would draw me up to Learner territory.

"This chart guides us to become much better observers of ourselves," Joseph said. "It lists Learner and Judger qualities and characteristics to help us discern where we are at any moment. It's invaluable for helping us strengthen our observer self and shift from Judger to Learner. Let's use it to do some personal research. Think about Charles. Then read off any words or phrases that leap to your attention."

"*Reactive and automatic. Know-it-all. Listening for agreement or disagreement. Self-righteous...*" I stopped. Everything I was reading was in the *Judger Mindset* column. My jaw

Learner/Judger Chart

Mindsets

Judger	Learner
Judgmental (of self and/or others)	Accepting (of self and others)
Reactive and automatic	Responsive and thoughtful
Blame	Responsibility
"Know-it-all"	Values not-knowing
Inflexible and rigid	Flexible and adaptive
Either/or thinking	Both/and thinking
Self-righteous	Inquisitive
Personal perspective only	Considers perspectives of others
Defends assumptions	Questions assumptions
Possibilities seen as limited	Possibilities seen as unlimited
Primary mood: protective	Primary mood: curious

We all have both mindsets, and we have the power to choose where we operate from in any moment.

Relationships

Judger	Learner
Win-lose relationships	Win-win relationships
Debates	Dialogues
Feels separate from others/self	Feels connected with others/self
Fears differences	Values differences
Feedback perceived as rejection	Feedback perceived as worthwhile
Listens for:	Listens for:
• Differences	• Commonalities
• Right/wrong	• Facts
• Agree/disagree	• Understanding
Seeks to attack or defend	Seeks to resolve and create

We all relate from both mindsets, and we have the power to choose how we relate in any moment.

tightened. Then I turned to the *Learner Mindset* column. Only one phrase caught my eye: *Values not-knowing.* I was puzzled.

"I'm not sure what you mean by *values not-knowing*," I said.

"It's like when someone is doing research," Joseph explained. "You want to discover something new, which is impossible if you're attached to the conviction that you already know all the answers. Valuing not-knowing is the basis of learning and all creativity and innovation. It's the state of mind that's open to all kinds of new possibilities and even hoping you might be surprised. Instead of defending old opinions or positions or answers, your goal is to look with fresh eyes. I like to think of this as 'rational humility,' a maturity we develop by admitting that it's impossible to ever have all the answers."

Rational humility! I liked that. That's how it felt when I was doing technological research. Beyond that, especially with relationships, I felt like I was in foreign territory. Suddenly, I was confused. *Was it Charles or me who was reactive and automatic? Was it Charles or me who was the know-it-all? Who was listening for agreement or disagreement? Who was self-righteous? Who was the big Judger here?*

Before I could recover from my confusion, Joseph hit me with a new question. "What do you think it costs you to spend so much time in the Judger Pit?"

"*Costs* me?" I said quietly, looking at Joseph and then at the floor. His question had hit me like a thunderbolt. "I don't even want to think about the cost to the company for my Judger habits. First of all, I'm getting a pretty good salary, but it's money down a black hole in terms of what I'm producing. On top of that, I'm starting to suspect that I've created a no-win situation that's brought my whole team down. I dread going to meetings with those people. And the trickle down to other departments we work with … well, this isn't a pretty picture!"

Joseph was nodding, apparently satisfied with my insights. "This is real progress," he told me. "You're doing great, Ben."

"Great? What are you talking about? This is a disaster. Throw me a lifeline, would you? How do I get out of this?"

"I *could* drag you out," Joseph said, "but I'm going to give you something even more valuable — tools to get yourself out. I'm a big believer in the 'teach 'em to fish' philosophy. Now, I want you to bring to mind a time when you were in Learner in a work situation. Got the picture? Recall as vividly as you can what that experience was like. If you have trouble remembering, take a look at the Learner side of the chart."

Right away I recalled my best work at KB Corp, how everything flowed, how I woke up every morning looking forward to going to work. My productivity was high. So was everybody else's. People even said they enjoyed working with me, though the truth is I spent a lot of time alone. I could feel myself smiling at the memory. My work life then couldn't have been any more different than the nightmare I was experiencing now.

"I just had a thought," I said. "At KB I didn't have to deal with people much except to come up with innovative answers to their technological questions. Under those circumstances, it wasn't such a challenge to stay in Learner."

"I see what you mean," Joseph said. "Applying those same principles to your present leadership role might be a challenge. Humans aren't machines."

"That's what my wife keeps telling me," I said.

We both chuckled.

"So let me see if I understand you correctly," Joseph said. "With technology problems, your Learner curiosity is natural and easy. You're really good at that. You have specific questions that help you step outside yourself, to make objective observations, and assess what's going on. In those situations, you understand that whatever you come up with is neither good nor bad — it's simply information. Thomas Edison was famous for telling people how it took thousands of failures to invent the electric light bulb, and that each failure contributed to that final successful solution.

"I'm giving you new tools to take advantage of what you already know how to do. When you can recognize Judger, distinguish it from Learner, and switch to Learner whenever you choose, you're well on your way to taking charge of your life — at work *and* at home."

Suddenly something clicked for me. I turned my attention to the Choice Map as Joseph spoke and focused on the Switching Lane. "Switching is what makes it possible to change," I exclaimed. "Switching is where the action is!"

Joseph nodded emphatically. "Yes! You've got it!"

> Switching is what makes it
> possible to change.
> Switching is where the action is!

he proclaimed. "The ability to switch literally puts you in charge of change. Being able to nonjudgmentally observe your own Judger and then ask a Switching question — well, that's about the most powerful and courageous thing anybody can do for themselves. It's the operational heart of change, what many people call *self-management*. Actually, combining the *willingness* and *ability* to switch leads not only to change, it also makes us able to *sustain* change, because we're observing and asking ourselves Learner questions moment by moment by moment. Switching mindsets can literally give us new eyes and new ears."

Joseph's enthusiasm was contagious. I was eager to learn more, especially the parts about change and *sustaining* change, and how that could help my results at work. But a glance at the clock told me it was time to end today's meeting.

| 7 | *Seeing with New Eyes,* *Hearing with New Ears* |

We started our next meeting with a question that had been disturbing me since early in my conversations with Joseph. "Maybe it's just wishful thinking," I began, "but given the problems Judger throws our way..."

Joseph lifted his hand, signaling me to stop, and replied, "None of us can avoid slipping into Judger from time to time. It's only human." Then he smiled enigmatically and added, "But you can *free yourself from Judger,* simply by accepting that part of yourself. Judger is not the problem, *it's how we relate to Judger* that makes all the difference. It's such a simple formula: *Judger-Switch-Learner*. But nobody can use it without beginning with acceptance."

"Huh? That doesn't make sense. How can I be free of something that's part of me?"

"It does sound like a paradox, doesn't it," Joseph said. "But it *is* possible. Simple acceptance of *what is* creates a level playing field so that change is really possible. But leveling the field can also be challenging, especially if Judger whispers in your ear a lot. Did Alexa ever tell you about her husband Stan's breakthrough?"

"She mentioned it," I replied. "You helped him make a pile of money, as I understand it."

"He's very proud of that story," Joseph said. "He used the QT tools to earn his way into my Hall of Fame. Stan, as Alexa may have told you, is in the investment business. Accepting his own Judger turned out to be very profitable for him!

"Some years back, Stan was a very judgmental guy. He didn't think of himself that way, but many people around him did. If he had a run-in with someone, or heard gossip about them that wasn't flattering, he'd just write them off. Stan will tell you that he clung to his assumptions and opinions like a bull terrier to a bone. He turned down many business opportunities on the basis of rumor, idle gossip, and guilt by association. He justified it all as a way of minimizing risk — which was only partially true.

"One time he made a huge investment in a promising start-up company. About a year later, the company hired a

CEO who'd been employed by a firm that was implicated in a big financial scandal. Although this new guy had been exonerated of any wrongdoing, Stan insisted that where there was smoke there was fire. He was on the verge of pulling his money out but was also in a great deal of conflict about the whole thing. Except for the CEO they'd hired, the company seemed to be doing everything right.

"About this time, Sarah and I had dinner with Stan and Alexa. We were discussing the Learner/Judger material and Alexa encouraged Stan to use Switching questions to evaluate his investment decision. She suggested he apply the *ABCC Choice Process* to that issue. That's the tool I've been promising to tell you about. Stan agreed to try it and he was amazed at what a big difference it made. Here's how the ABCC Choice Process works:

"*A — Aware. Am I in Judger?* Stan was very funny about this. After we described the characteristics of Judger, Stan, amazingly, admitted that an awful lot of what we described applied to him. His response surprised us: 'Being in Judger is my forte!' We all laughed, though we knew he was beginning to look at his behavior more honestly.

"*B — Breathe! Do I need to pause, step back, and look at this situation more objectively?* Stan smiled at this question, took a deep breath, paused, and shortly admitted that he was being anything but objective, especially because so much money was involved. He really distrusted this new CEO, though he'd never even spoken with the man.

ABCC Choice Process

A   **Aware**
Am I in Judger?

B   **Breathe**
Do I need to step back, pause, and look at this situation more objectively?

C   **Curiosity**
Do I have all the facts? What's happening here?

C   **Choose**
What's my choice?

"*C — Curiosity. What's happening here? What are the facts?* We asked Stan if he'd done anything to collect objective information. Did he have everything he needed to make a responsible judgment? Stan realized that he'd never gotten past his distaste for what he'd heard about the guy. But facts? No, he actually had no facts.

"*C — Choose. What's my choice?* Well, by then Stan himself realized that he didn't have all the information he needed to make a wise choice. Because of his investment he owed it to himself to check things out. A month later Stan called to tell me he'd checked around and found out the new CEO was a good guy. Long story short, Stan left his money in, the company went public two years later, and he made a fortune.

"The whole situation made Stan stop and think. It was a real wake-up call for him. Having realized how much money his Judger almost cost him, Stan tells me he uses ABCC all the time. He even jokes that he's starting to hard-wire those questions into his brain! None of this would have happened if he hadn't been able to simply accept and observe the Judger part of himself. Using this process begins with awareness and acceptance, then builds on it. Stan certainly reaped the rewards!

"If you met Stan today, you'd still notice that he can be opinionated and judgmental. He knows that part of himself very well and accepts it, but now he doesn't allow it to blind him in making decisions. He even has a sense of humor about his Judger."

"Great story!" I said, and I really meant it. I found the ABCC formula in my workbook and jotted down a few notes.

"Think about Stan making all that money and my wife finally being successful with her weight," Joseph noted. "If either of them had wasted time being judgmental about their own Judger, they wouldn't have gotten to first base in making the changes they wanted."

"This all sounds great. It really does. But here's something I'm stuck on. Learner can sound soft. Leaders have to be strong and decisive. Leaders have to act tough and make tough calls. I don't see how being more of a Learner can help me do that."

"How about Alexa," Joseph countered. "How does she handle the tough calls?"

"Point made," I responded quickly, thinking back to some difficult decisions she had made that I wouldn't have wanted to face myself. She could be tough as nails when the situation demanded it, yet I still felt respected even when she challenged me.

Joseph continued, "There's an important difference between 'Learner tough' and 'Judger tough.' You can get the job done from either position. However, a Learner leader displays the kind of toughness that builds loyalty and respect as well as cooperation and risk-taking. Judger leaders are more likely to generate fear, distrust, and conflict around them."

Was Joseph referring to my leadership style and nightmare team? Rather than bringing that up, I challenged him about another reservation I had about Learner.

"Doesn't Learner slow things down?" I asked. "Work is just one pressure and deadline after another. Sometimes I'm staggered by the amount of things I need to do and how fast they have to happen. If I had to be in Learner all the time, wouldn't it take forever to get things done? I mean, wouldn't I end up more behind than ever?"

Joseph just answered my question with more of his own.

"How many times, when you were in a rush, have you made a mistake, blamed yourself or others, and then had to do it all over? How much extra time did *that* take? In your haste, how many times have you been impatient or impolite to someone and then noticed that he or she didn't talk to you much after that? What's the cost in time, results, and even loyalty when you treat people like that?"

I just stared at him. It felt like he had been watching me in my office all day long, five days a week. Then he added, "That's what happens when Judger takes over at work. On the other hand, I've heard over and over from the folks in my Question Thinking Hall of Fame that Learner actually helps them *save time* as well as be more productive."

"That's impressive," I said. "It sure seems like life would be a lot simpler if we could all just recognize and accept Judger in ourselves, switch to Learner, and operate from there."

"How true!" Joseph said. "That's one of the ultimate goals of Question Thinking. Imagine what work would be like if people did this most of the time. You would have a Learner culture; you could even call yours a Learner organization. And what about your team, Ben? The one you complain about so much. Are they in Judger or Learner most of the time? As the leader of the team, *your* results will only get better if *theirs* do." He paused for a moment, then added: "Think of all we've been discussing as a *practice*, something you pay attention to daily, sometimes hour by hour, sometimes moment by moment. You'll soon be seeing with new eyes and hearing with new ears."

Seeing with New Eyes, Hearing with New Ears

Joseph glanced at his watch. "We've been talking quite a while. We can take a short break and then go onto the next step, or wait until the next time we get together. What do you want to do?"

I was torn. I needed time to digest what we'd covered so far. But frankly, I was eager to hear the rest of what Joseph would tell me. I knew it would help with conversations that would soon be coming up with Charles — and also with Grace. It took only a second to make my decision. "Okay, let's go for it!"

Learner Teams and Judger Teams

8

During our break, I started remembering what it had been like to work at KB. It had been very different from what I was now experiencing at QTec. When I compared the two experiences — KB versus QTec — there wasn't a doubt in my mind that at KB I had mostly been in Learner. As a research engineer I did most of my work alone, then reported my findings to the team, taking their questions and providing answers. It was easy to be in Learner most of the time. By contrast, at QTec it was apparent that I was in Judger more often than I cared to admit. No matter where I looked, especially with my team, something seemed to be going wrong or some-body was failing to do what they were supposed to. How could I avoid going into Judger? As Joseph and I continued our meeting that day, I hesitantly shared this observation with him and told him, "I'm not sure where to take it from here."

"I think I can best respond to that with a story," Joseph replied. "You've probably heard of the mythologist Joseph Campbell. He was famous for coming up with exactly the right story for every situation. Here's one I heard many years ago.

"It seems a farmer was out working his field when his plow caught on something that wouldn't budge. His first reaction, of course, was to go into Judger. Cursing, he began digging around to free the plow. To his surprise, it was caught on an iron ring buried deep in the ground.

"After freeing his plow, the farmer got curious and pulled on the iron ring. Off came the lid of an ancient chest. Before him, glittering in the sun lay a treasure of precious jewels and gold.

"This story reminds us that it is often by confronting our toughest obstacles that we find our greatest strengths and possibilities, but sometimes we've got to dig deep to find them. Campbell had a phrase for it: *Where you stumble, there your treasure is.* You'd ask yourself questions like *What could I discover? What might be valuable here?*"

"That might be fine and well. But I'm still not seeing

> # Where you stumble,
> # there your treasure is.
> ## *Joseph Campbell*

how all this is going to help me. Where's the treasure in this mess of mine?"

Joseph easily took up my challenge. "How about doing a little excavating," he said. "To start with, let's look at how your questions affect people around you." He leaned back in his chair and took a deep breath. "Let's look at your team. How often are you in Judger when you meet with them?"

"Truthfully? Just about every meeting lately!"

"And how would you say you communicate with the members of your team?"

"Communicate? That's a laugh! Listen, I told you how awful our meetings are. When I do call a meeting nobody has much to offer. They sit on their hands and wait for me to tell them what to do. Finally I talk and Charles barrages me with his interminable questions. Doesn't matter what I say, he questions everything."

"Think of yourself as the farmer in Campbell's story," Joseph continued. "When you're with your team, are you cursing the fact that your plow got stuck or are you curious about finding the door to the treasure? Are you looking for who's to blame or are you looking for what's working? Are you asking yourself questions like, *How can I show them I have the right answer?* Or are you asking, *What can we accomplish together?*"

I wasn't sure what I did but I knew it wasn't what Joseph was suggesting. "I guess you'll have to clue me in here."

"Okay. You've been in conferences with Alexa. How does she conduct her meetings? What does she say and do? How do her meetings affect you?"

"I look forward to Alexa's meetings," I told Joseph. "They're always exciting. I come away with new ideas to pursue. I feel like charging back to my office to start acting on them. But I never could figure out what she does to generate that kind of excitement."

The moment those words were out of my mouth, it hit me. "Alexa asks questions," I said. "Her meetings are all about questions. But not interrogating kinds of questions. She really piques everyone's curiosity. Her questions motivate us, sometimes even inspire us."

Joseph sat back in his chair a moment before leaning forward enthusiastically. "Alexa's questions send you away wanting to contribute your best. She inspires people to abandon Judger and operate from Learner. She likes to say that 'Learner begets Learner. And Judger begets Judger.' You could even call Alexa a Learner leader." Joseph paused for a moment and then asked, "How do you think her questions are different from yours?"

> ## Learner begets Learner and Judger begets Judger.

"Alexa has her style, I have mine," I said, getting a little defensive.

"Do you ask questions?"

"Sure I ask questions. I ask my people what they've accomplished since our previous meetings. Or what they haven't, which is more accurate lately."

"When they answer, how do you listen? How do you respond?"

"It depends. If the answer is any good, I might jot it down. But lately, I leave those meetings with a blank pad."

"Describe what the experience of listening is like for you," Joseph said.

That wasn't difficult. "Mostly I've been pretty annoyed and impatient," I replied, "especially when a person's answer doesn't come close to solving the problem, or when it shows they're not following my plan. I get the impression nobody really cares."

"In situations like those, what's your attitude toward your colleagues? Are you in Learner or Judger most of the time?"

"What else! Judger, of course. But nobody is contributing a darn thing...if they would only..."

Joseph held up his hand. "Whoa! Hold on, my friend. When you're with your team, it sounds like you're listening with Judger questions like, *Are they going to screw up again?* and *How are they going to disappoint me this time?*"

"Sure, those sound like my questions. Based on my experience with them, what else would I be asking?" I suddenly stopped. "Boy, I just stubbed my toe on the iron ring in the story you just told me, didn't I?"

"You sure did. Good observation! And like the farmer, your first reaction was to go Judger — which is natural enough," Joseph said. "Now do what the farmer did after that. Get curious. Ask yourself, 'What's happening here?' Think about your team and this time follow the Learner Path."

"Follow the Learner Path with my team? You've got to be kidding," I said. "Besides, how would I do that?"

"For starters, reset yourself in Learner mindset before you meet with your team. Try the kinds of questions Alexa asks, like, *What do I appreciate about them? What are the best strengths of each one of them? How can I help them collaborate most productively? How can we stay on the Learner Path together?*

"I'll bet you can see how those Learner questions would change everything in a meeting. Alexa's questions create a Learner environment. They invite everyone — including you — to listen more patiently and carefully. With Learner questions we listen in order to understand the other person rather than to find out who's right or wrong. That makes it possible for everyone to get curious, feel safe taking risks, and participate fully, even when they're facing tough challenges."

"It's the tough challenges part that gets me in trouble," I argued. "We've got some big problems and nobody is willing to speak up, much less take them on. Plus, there are so many major decisions we disagree on. We just can't seem to get through the conflicts to the other side. That's when I get frustrated and start feeling like nothing is ever going to work out. I think myself right down into the Judger Pit."

"Even though you'll never be pure Learner, including with your team, you can learn to choose where you put your attention moment to moment. Any attention you give to Judger isn't available to give to Learner. Accept Judger, practice Learner. Imprint that slogan on your brain. It's as important for teams as it is for individuals."

> ## Any attention you give to Judger isn't available to give to Learner.

"That's why Alexa's meetings are so great," I reflected. "They're Learner environments, like you say. I always have the sense that we have her full attention and that she really cares about what we have to say. If she ever goes Judger, I'm sure it's just for a fleeting visit." I had a sudden insight. "*All* she asks are Learner questions, and lots of them. Plus, I'll bet she gets an almost perfect score on that rule you told me about. You know, *much more* asking, much *less* telling. That's why she's called the *inquiring leader*, isn't it?"

> ## Accept Judger and practice Learner. It's as important for teams as for individuals!

"That's it," Joseph said. "Alexa genuinely cares about what people have to say. Not only does she ask Learner questions, she also listens with Learner ears. Alexa's listening is focused by questions such as: *What's valuable here? What's to be learned from that comment? How can this contribute to what we're working on?* The questions she listens with help her teams turn into Learner teams very quickly. She expects to find the treasure, she looks for it, and much of the time she finds it.

"The Choice Map can help you do this with your team, too. Look at it again. So far, we've been thinking about it as a guide for how an *individual* thinks, behaves, and relates. Now, let's consider it as a guide for *teams*. Start thinking in terms of *Learner teams* and *Judger teams*.

"I think of Learner teams as being typically high performing, and Judger teams as being typically low performing. When researchers explored what distinguished high-performing teams from low-performing ones, can you guess what they found?"

Part of me didn't even want to know; another part was intrigued. But I decided not to guess. "No, what?" I replied.

"First of all, the high-performing teams had more positive emotions than the low-performing ones. That's not a big surprise. But what I found revealing was that the low-performing teams were low on *inquiry* — that is, on asking questions — and high on *advocacy* — that is, on pushing a particular viewpoint rather than listening to anybody else."

"So the bottom line," I said, "is if you want high performance, focus on Learner."

"Yes," Joseph said. "But there's more. The research also showed that high-performing teams consistently had a good balance between inquiry and advocacy. That has to have been *Learner* inquiry and *Learner* advocacy. It means that people feel free to ask tough questions and have genuine open debate. They can even argue and have conflicts, yet the atmosphere remains Learner."

"That's exactly what happens with Alexa's meetings," I said. "This is great!"

"It's what Alexa calls a Learner Alliance," Joseph said. "It's when team members work together to stay on the Learner Path. That's completely opposite of what happens when members of a team go Judger. They would end up in what I call a *Judger stand-off*. Everyone just defends their own position and doesn't listen to any other ideas. Nothing

> **Learner Alliance:** When team members work together to stay on the Learner Path

gets done and everyone blames someone else. That's the real cost of Judger when it takes over a team."

When I pictured the Choice Map I could clearly imagine Alexa's whole team jogging happily along the Learner Path, set off on their journey with Learner questions. Their attention was free to focus on new solutions and possibilities. Alexa's team would certainly qualify as a high-performing one. And my team? Most of my people were down at the bottom of the map, mired in the mud of the Judger Pit—and I'd put them there! I hated to admit this. But accepting it was the only way I'd ever get them out.

"I'm just the opposite of Alexa," I mumbled. "She seems to create a balanced Learner environment almost automatically."

"She wasn't always that way. Like most of us," Joseph noted, "she was automatically more Judger to start with. It usually takes effort and intention to turn the tide and become more naturally Learner. Think about it as deliberately training your brain to do things it doesn't automatically know how to do. Like anything—learning to drive a car or operate a computer or learning to ride a bike—it requires close attention at first, but soon becomes second nature."

"This is a lot to take in," I said. "When I first walked into your office, truthfully I was just looking for a quick fix. What you're offering is obviously a lot bigger."

Joseph nodded.

"Can't you narrow it down to a few words of advice?" I joked.

"How often do people really take advice?"

He was right, of course. "I guess I'm an expert at *not taking* advice." I grinned at my sudden insight.

"Aren't we all?" Joseph replied. "Even though it's hard to resist, I try to avoid giving advice. I know that if I ask good questions, people are smart enough to come up with their own best answers. Our own advice is the only kind most of us listen to and act on anyway...but I do have a suggestion for you, Ben." Joseph flashed his signature mischievous grin. "Do you want to hear it?"

"Sure," I said — and we both laughed.

"Alexa is a great model for what you and I are working on. She personally went through a lot of similar things as you to accomplish what she has. Next time you meet with Alexa, ask her to tell you about that. I'm sure she'd be happy to."

Good suggestion! I thought. Then I asked Joseph if there were any other things I should bring up with Alexa.

Joseph nodded. "There is something else. Alexa came up with this terrific Question Thinking practice she calls

Q-Storming. It's sort of like brainstorming except that you're looking for new questions instead of answers and ideas. Ask her to explain Q-Storming to you. There's also a tool about it in your workbook. Alexa credits it with being the catalyst for many of her most important breakthroughs."

Now that sounded really intriguing — and promising. That's where we ended our conversation that day.

Down on the street a few minutes later, I cut through the park across from the Pearl Building into an open playing field where an older boy was helping a younger one learn to ride his bicycle. I stopped to watch.

In spite of spills and near falls, they were having fun. There were shouts of encouragement, along with cries of despair as the younger boy made yet another mistake and tumbled to the ground. Each time the younger boy fell, the older one rushed to his side to give assistance and support to try again.

Finally, the younger boy caught on. He rode off, covering 50 feet or so, with the older boy chasing after him, whooping and hollering cries of victory. I caught myself thinking, *Why are adults so damned competitive? Why are they so uncooperative, always looking for ways to show up the other guy? Why did I have to put up with people like Charles?* I was getting angry. I turned around to catch one last glimpse of the kids before getting into my car. Now the two of them were standing beside the upright bike, laughing together. I reached for the ignition and thought, *Wouldn't it be amazing*

*if our team could work together just like those kids? I wonder
what it would take to make that happen?*

At that moment I realized I'd done something that
was still quite new for me. I had transformed Judger questions into Learner ones. *Not bad*, I thought. I couldn't wait
to share this with Joseph. That's when it occurred to me
that maybe I really could follow Alexa's example — turn
my team into a Learner team by becoming a Learner leader.
The inquiring coach, as Alexa called Joseph, was really onto
something! I wanted to find out what else Joseph had up his
sleeve. I was beginning to feel real hope that maybe it wasn't
too late to salvage my career.

9 | *When the Magic Works*

Over breakfast a few days later, Grace told me about what had happened with Jennifer, the young woman she'd been having so much trouble with at work. Grace even apologized for calling me during the day just to vent.

"I kept the Choice Map on my desk all day," Grace said. "Two Learner questions kept jumping out at me — *What do I want?* and *What are my choices?* When I applied those questions to Jennifer, I realized I wanted her to start showing more common sense and initiative. So, I tried some new questions. I asked myself, *Why does Jennifer need so much direction from me?* I became truly curious after I realized I didn't know. Was she afraid of acting on her own? Or worried that I'd fire her for making a mistake? I also wondered whether she had more going for her than I'd given her credit for. The next time she came to me for help I asked her a question instead of just giving her instructions. I inquired, 'How would you solve this problem if you were the boss?'

"That single question opened up a very productive conversation. Jennifer confessed that she was, indeed, afraid of me. She thought if she didn't do exactly what I expected her to, I'd fire her. This is what had happened with her previous boss and she didn't want it to ever happen again. That talk changed everything between us. She said she felt better about taking initiative and working on her own. She also came up with some good ideas for solving her own problem. She was obviously very pleased with herself. I congratulated her — and told her how happy I was that we had our talk.

"I'm really surprised, and glad. And, you know what? Asking Learner questions made me feel a lot better at the end of the day. I realize now I was being unfair to Jennifer. I had been assuming she was asking all those questions because she was incompetent. She really isn't. It's just that she believed she had to check everything out with me before acting on her own."

As Grace told me the story of her breakthrough with Jennifer, I was relieved she didn't ask me about any results I'd gotten from working with Joseph's ideas. It's true I'd had some shifts in my thinking and was somewhat hopeful rather than resigned. But I didn't have much to show for my efforts yet. And my team was still a nightmare.

When I finally left home I was at least twenty minutes late. Traffic was piling up on the freeway. A mile past my on-ramp, the highway turned into a parking lot. Cars were lined up as far as I could see, four lanes wide. I was getting frantic. I didn't even notice how much my Judger mindset had kicked in. At least not right away.

Then traffic stopped completely. I gritted my teeth, set the car in park, and pulled out my cell phone to check for messages. My secretary had left several reminders, which did nothing to lessen my stress. I was already anxious about that morning's meeting with Alexa and was dreading the one with Charles that afternoon. I wasn't ready for either, least of all the latter.

I slapped the steering wheel in frustration, muttering something about how one guy, stupid enough to run out of gas, had ruined the whole day for half the city. *Who was the idiot responsible? I didn't need this! Didn't he realize…* I suddenly stopped myself. I was solidly in Judger! I actually laughed out loud. Then I heard sirens and an ambulance sped along the emergency lane toward the front of the line. Accident! I switched on the radio for traffic news. Two people badly injured. I felt pretty foolish about jumping to the conclusion that some jerk had run out of gas.

As I sat in my car fuming, worries about my meeting

with Charles kept intruding. My thoughts were going round and round, fueled by my anger with him. I sure needed help with this one. What would Joseph tell me? I heard his voice in my head, reminding me how important it is to change my questions, especially with Charles and my team. Yesterday he'd told me to find a real situation to test out what I'd been learning. This upcoming meeting with Charles was about as real as it gets. But what questions would help me get out of what Grace called a *Judger-head?* What Learner questions could help Charles and me get off to a good start? Traffic suddenly moved forward a hundred yards or so before it stopped again. In those few moments I realized I had already stepped onto the Switching Lane with the questions I'd just asked myself.

Joseph kept suggesting that whenever I caught myself in Judger I should stop, take a deep breath, and go into observer to find out what I was asking myself at that moment. I did that. The first one that popped into my mind was about the traffic jam: *How can I get out of here?* Obviously, there wasn't much choice about that. I was stuck until traffic started moving again. Then something else Joseph said came back to me: I don't have much control over what happens, but I can *choose* how I relate to what happens. Almost immediately, a new question came to mind: *How can I make best use of this time?*

It took only a second to come up with an answer to that one. I fished my wallet out of my pocket, took out Joseph's business card, and punched his number into my cell phone. He answered immediately.

"Ben here," I said. "Do you have a minute? I'm stuck in traffic and going a little nuts."

Joseph was silent for a moment, then laughed: "Did you try saying *beam me up Scotty?*"

"How'd you know I was such a Trekkie," I laughed too and almost instantly my mood lightened.

"I've got a meeting with Charles this afternoon," I explained. "I realize I have to get into Learner mindset to even have a chance of it going well. I'm worried that I'll blow it. Where do I begin?"

"Good question," Joseph said. "Can you write something down?"

"Sure," I said. "Go ahead."

As I sat there stalled in traffic, Joseph dictated three questions: *What assumptions am I making? How else can I think about this?* And, *What is the other person thinking, feeling, and wanting?*" Joseph explained that these questions were from his *Top Twelve Questions for Success*, one of the tools in the workbook.

I looked at the first question: *What assumptions am I making?* That was easy enough. Where Charles was concerned my assumptions were unavoidable. I'd beaten him out of a big promotion. Guys in that position can be dangerous. I'd be a fool to drop my guard with him. I was sure nothing would make Charles happier than to see me fail. I was also sure he'd do whatever he could to make that happen. Then he could step into my position and have what he

Ben's Three Questions

1 What assumptions am I making?

2 How else can I think about this?

3 What is the other person thinking, feeling, and wanting?

wanted. Who wouldn't assume you had to watch your back with guys like that?

Sure, these were just assumptions. I wasn't denying that. But there are situations where going with your assumptions is the safest route, and this was one of them. So far, the problems I was having with Charles seemed real enough to me.

As I thought about all this, something I'd read in the Learner/Judger Chart kept nagging at me: *Was I defending my assumptions instead of questioning them?*

Though still unsettled, I turned to Joseph's second question: *How else can I think about this?* Something Grace had said clicked in my mind — how her assumptions about Jennifer had damaged their relationship. Grace had used the Choice Map to find a different way of relating to Jennifer. Could I do the same with Charles?

I began to wonder about other possibilities. For example, what would happen if I reconsidered some of my opinions about Charles? What if I tried on the assumption that his questions weren't aimed at making me look bad? What if he just wanted to make sure we'd covered all our bases? Then I remembered Joseph telling me about winning teams and their balance between inquiry and advocacy. What if Charles's endless questions were just his way to encourage more thoughtful discussions in our meetings? I was pretty sure I was giving Charles more credit than he was due — but maybe not. The more I considered other ways of thinking about the situation, the less certain I was about my old opinions.

I decided to try something new in my meeting with Charles that afternoon. When he walked in, I would suspend thinking that he was after my job and out to sabotage me. The moment this thought crossed my mind, new ideas tumbled into place. I wasn't ready to totally trust Joseph's theories but I was ready to give Charles the benefit of the doubt. This was great. I actually had something new and useful to *do*.

I was just starting to consider Joseph's third question — *What is the other person thinking, feeling, and wanting?* — when traffic began to inch forward. I put that question on hold. But even as I got under way, new possibilities began unfolding in my mind. If Charles was merely being inquisitive, what was he wanting or needing from me? I remembered a conversation we'd had my first day on the job. He'd said, "I have to tell you, I'm disappointed I didn't get the promotion. This is a great company and my family likes this town. I don't want to have to move them. I'll do everything I can to make this company successful."

His comment that he'd do anything to make this company successful still bothered me. What exactly did he mean by that? My assumption had been that this included going after my job. Could I have misread Charles's intentions?

I arrived at my office way behind schedule. With less than ten minutes before my meeting with Alexa, I sat down at my computer, typed in her name and that of the magazine I'd seen in Joseph's Hall of Fame collection. The article about her popped up instantly.

Fast Company Magazine had chosen Alexa for their *Woman of the Year* award before we'd ever met at KB. I scanned the story. It told about her stepping into the CEO position of a company that had already gone into Chapter 11. Everyone had advised her against it. They said it could destroy her career. She took the risk and accomplished the impossible. I skipped ahead several paragraphs. Alexa was quoted as saying she owed her success to "simply changing the kinds of questions I was asking." In the next paragraph she named her personal coach and mentor: Joseph S. Edwards. Who else?

Moments after reading the article, I was seated in Alexa's office. Although my intention was to ask her about Q-Storming, my curiosity got the best of me and I found myself asking about the *Fast Company* article. "You never told me about your getting the *Woman of the Year* award," I said. "I just read about it on the Internet."

"Oh, yes. They labeled me *The Inquiring Leader*. You know what? I don't think my interviewer had ever heard of a CEO making a point of asking lots of questions. It was a great novelty to him!" She chuckled at the thought. "It seems like such a simple thing. Most leaders do more telling than asking. That's why they never find out what's really going on. All too often they base their decisions about strategic direction, and even about their own people, on insufficient or inaccurate information."

"They make assumptions instead," I added, "which they never test."

"Exactly. Well, that just never made any sense to me."

I heard Joseph's teachings in her words, but what she said was obviously authentic for her.

"Joseph and I have been discussing Learner and Judger mindsets and the Choice Map," I said. "He told me I'm not the only person in this room who ever ran into problems with Judger." I checked to make sure she didn't mind my saying that. She was smiling, so I continued. "He suggested you might share some of your own Judger challenges with your old company. What were some of the Judger questions you started out with?"

"You know, in retrospect it seems so simple I almost laugh. The kinds of questions I'd been asking were along the order of, *Who's to blame for the mess we're in?* I was lying awake nights trying to figure out whom I should fire — and worrying that it might be myself! Then, one day, working with Joseph, I started coming up with new questions. I think the first one was, *How can we avoid making so many mistakes?* Joseph thought that was a good beginning but suggested I could come up with something even better."

"You mean a stronger Learner question?"

"Exactly," Alexa said. "The one I figured out was, *How can we build on our strengths and successes?* I really took that question seriously and started asking it all the time. I got everyone on track with that new question. I could see that the Judger questions I'd been asking made everything more difficult. Judger drained our energy, pretty much killed our enthusiasm, divided us so we were always looking for someone to blame — in short, Judger derailed us and had us going in all directions at once, none of which were very productive. That new Learner question piqued our curiosity and invited us to take positive, focused, and creative actions together. Joseph said to use those new questions to build a Learner environment, and that's what I set out to do. Pretty soon we were turning things around in remarkable ways. Until then, I'd never really gotten the truth about the power of questions, that they can lead us to failure or to success. It really was a big change for me, and for all of us."

"What was it about that new question that made such a difference?" I asked.

"Maybe an example Joseph gave us would make this

clearer. It had to do with a study that was done with two comparable bowling teams. Team A was coached with an emphasis on preventing mistakes when they bowled. Day after day, they reviewed videos that focused on their errors. Those mistakes got grooved in their brains. By contrast, Team B was coached with an emphasis on building on their successes. Day after day, they reviewed videos that focused on their most successful moves. So Team B's successes got grooved in their brains.

"To put it simply, Team A focused on what was wrong. Team B focused on what was right. I'm sure you can guess which team had the greatest improvement in their total scores."

"The one that built on their successes, of course."

"That's absolutely right," Alexa said. "In fact, by the end, the difference in these teams' performances was startling. As I recall, Team A actually had a slight reduction in their accomplishments. Team B improved by nearly 30 percent. That's all it took to convince me of the power of asking the right kinds of questions. I applied those same principles to our floundering company and that's when dramatic changes began to occur. Not only did our productivity increase but coming to work was more enjoyable, even fun. Creativity and mood were boosted. There was higher energy throughout the company. The whole place began operating on Learner principles and shifting to Learner questions — the way that Learner begets Learner — and it all happened in months instead of years. I guess you just read the rest of the story."

Alexa paused as she recalled that time of her life. "What could be more natural or obvious," she continued, "than to *simply ask*? How else can you get a complete picture of what's going on? How else can you get people contributing so enthusiastically? Could we ever discover or learn or create anything new without being curious first? Curiosity is one of our greatest assets. I'm sure Joseph has emphasized this to you. Curiosity is the fast track to Learner. It's hightest fuel for change and progress!"

Curiosity is the fast track to Learner.

As Alexa talked, I was thinking about how important it was to check my assumptions about Charles. *Were my Judger questions blinding me from seeing something important about him? Did I really know why Charles asked so many questions?* Before I had a chance to stop myself the words popped out of my mouth.

"He's just asking me all those questions because he's curious. He wants to understand!"

Alexa looked at me with concern. "What in heaven's name are you talking about?"

"Sorry, Alexa, I was just thinking out loud," I replied.

"This conversation has really gotten me all fired up about my team and our project."

"It sure seems that you're onto something," Alexa said, nodding her head. "And I think I can say with confidence that your new questions are going to produce some real progress."

My mind ran back to the conversation Grace and I had had earlier that morning. In working out her situation with Jennifer, Grace had started by asking herself, *What do I want?* and *What are my choices?* and then asked *How can I understand her?* I realized this last question wasn't one I asked myself about people I worked with. Instantly, other questions popped into my mind: How did anyone ever understand anyone else? Joseph claimed you started by getting curious about them. And then you asked them questions. This is exactly what Grace had done with Jennifer. What did I really understand about Charles? I began to feel my curiosity growing and realized I was naturally coming up with new questions about him.

I remembered that old question I'd reported to Joseph so proudly, *How can I prove I'm right?* Now I saw how that question had contributed to the team's perception of me as a know-it-all. By changing my question from *How can I prove I'm right?* to *How can I understand?* I was already beginning to see Charles in a whole new light. What a contrast there was not only between those two questions but also in my mood and in how I was thinking about Charles!

Suddenly I remembered about Q-Storming. "Before I forget," I said. "Joseph suggested I ask you about

Q-Storming. He said it was responsible for some of the best breakthroughs in your career."

Alexa's eyebrows went up. She sat forward and smiled. "It's one of my favorite subjects," she said. "You've heard of brainstorming, I'm sure. Q-Storming is like that, except you're looking for new questions, not for answers. It's a great way to get everyone on the same page, to think collaboratively and out of the box. I've used it to get new thinking for all kinds of reasons — for decision making, problem solving, innovation, and even conflict resolution. I've mostly used it with groups and teams but I've also discovered how helpful it can be in one-on-one conversations."

At that moment, the phone rang on Alexa's desk. "I may have to take this," she said. "I told my secretary not to interrupt us unless a certain call came in." She reached across the desk, picked up the phone, pressed it to her ear, and exchanged a few words with her receptionist. Then she shrugged apologetically and covered the receiver as she told me it was indeed the call she'd been waiting for.

On the way back to my office, I was disappointed that I hadn't been able to hear more about Q-Storming. And I was eager to learn more. Alexa seemed like living proof that there really was some magic in Joseph's theories. Was a little of it starting to rub off on me, too? That day still held some surprises, and the person who would coach me through Q-Storming was to be the biggest surprise of all.

10 | *Q-Storming to the Rescue*

With less than half an hour to get ready for my appointment with Charles, I focused on the three questions Joseph had given me that morning: *What assumptions am I making? How else might I think about this?* and *What is the other person thinking, feeling, and wanting?*

Then my secretary buzzed, announcing Charles's arrival. In the past, I would have kept him waiting. Today, I immediately got up and met him at the door. We shook hands, and I asked him how he was doing. He replied that he was fine but he looked a little nervous. At least I wasn't the only one. When I originally made the appointment with him, I'd been all set for a showdown. But that was before my meetings with Joseph. Since then, my perspective on the problems between us had changed considerably. I offered him a comfortable chair and asked if he'd like coffee or anything to drink. That must have surprised him because I'd never done that in the past. He thanked me but said he was fine, holding up a small bottle of water he'd brought along.

Yesterday while thinking about this meeting, I'd reviewed many of the things I'd learned from Joseph. I also considered details about how both Joseph and Alexa conducted their meetings with me. They had both asked lots of questions but they also had a certain way of speaking that put me at ease. I felt like they were always on my side, like they wanted me to succeed. When I thought about it, I realized that each of them made our meetings a Learner experience.

I'd recalled, for example, that Joseph made sure there wasn't a desk or other physical barrier between us. This always had the effect of putting me at ease, so I decided to try the same thing with Charles. With so much at stake, I wanted to take every opportunity to make this conversation successful. I slid my desk chair over so that Charles and I were sitting just a few feet apart near the window. He looked a bit apprehensive at first but seemed to grow a little more at ease as we went along.

"I'm very worried about how our team is doing," I began. "In fact, we're really in trouble. So I'd like to talk some things through with you. And if it's okay, can we start with a few questions?"

Charles stared back at me with a slightly worried expression, nodding slowly.

"Let me be quite candid with you," I continued, trying to think how Joseph would say this. "I've realized that I may have contributed to some of the problems we've been having with our team. I want to change that and I believe the place to start is with you and me."

I paused, checking out Charles's reaction. As far as I could tell, he was attentive and engaged, though he didn't look very relaxed. When I put myself in his place, it was easy to imagine what might be going through his mind. I continued: "I've made certain judgments about you that I now believe were a wrong interpretation. For example, I knew you'd been at QTec for several years and that you were in line for the job that was given to me. I'm pretty sure my arrival wasn't exactly good news for you, and I assumed you'd have trouble working under me. Am I right about this?"

Charles nodded. "I've got to confess that has been difficult. Alexa broke it to me gently enough, but that only goes so far."

His response surprised me. Had he already recognized the problem... and had he actually been working on it? It appeared so. For a moment I got defensive and guarded, thinking that if this were so maybe he should have gotten my job.

"Had the situation been reversed, I'd have been pretty bent out of shape myself," I said.

"I'm still working it out," Charles admitted. "Let me ask you this — *How am I doing?*"

"Considering that I put an awful lot off on you that really didn't belong on your shoulders, I think you're doing great."

"I'm not sure I understand," Charles said.

It wasn't easy saying what I did after that: "I made a few assumptions about you, Charles. First, I assumed that because I was brought in over you that you'd resent me and wouldn't be able to work with me. I realize I was judging you unfairly. My second assumption had to do with all those questions you ask in our meetings."

"My questions?" Charles looked totally bewildered, then gathered his thoughts enough to say, "I don't get it. Why would my questions be a problem? You're the new guy. I need to find out what you want, where you're going to take us. How else would I find out what I don't know if I don't ask?"

"Oh, I agree," I said. I wasn't ready to admit to him that I'd thought his questions were aimed at showing others on the team that I didn't have all the right answers. However, I did tell him that my job at QTec required a huge shift from the way I was accustomed to operating. "At my old company," I explained, "people came to me for answers. I was so good at it that I earned a sterling reputation as the Answer

Man. Here at QTec I'm heading up a team and I need other people to help me find answers."

Charles took a sip of water from his bottle, then said, "A few weeks before you came aboard, Alexa brought in this guy for a training session. It was about just this sort of thing, about questions and answers. He talked about the powerful impact of questions, how they can help us be more innovative and change our thinking, our relationships, and even an entire organization. He asked us how anyone could expect to get the best answers without *first* asking the best questions. One thing he said stands out in my memory. It was, *Great results begin with great questions.*"

I remembered Alexa telling me about that training the day she hired me. She explained how she was having Joseph come in to facilitate a core training on Question Thinking. She'd invited me to attend but I'd had a scheduling conflict and couldn't make it. Besides, I was the Answer Man! Questions didn't much interest me back then. That had been the first reference she ever made to Joseph, and since I hadn't yet met him, his name hadn't meant much to me. There was no doubt in my mind that Charles was describing Joseph's training, so it seemed safe to assume he also had some familiarity with Question Thinking and the Learner and Judger mindset material.

When he finished talking, I told Charles I had a question for him.

"Sure," he said.

131

Q-Storming to the Rescue

"How do we get past what's been blocking us and our team?" I asked. This was a question I'd come up with in my preparations for this meeting. "As you know, it's the eleventh hour for our project. If we don't get off the dime and move forward, we're up the creek. In particular, what do *you* need to help us be successful?"

For a moment, Charles seemed taken aback. Then he said, "I'm not sure I have an immediate answer, but I'll think about it. However, I am sure that whatever we're doing in this conversation is a whole lot better than it has been. It seems like a good direction." He paused, then added, "May I make a suggestion? I think I've got something that could be helpful to us."

My hackles went up. *Here he goes again*, I thought. He's going to challenge my authority. But I stopped myself quickly. In an instant three Self-Q's popped into my mind: *Am I in Judger? How else can I think about this? What do I want to accomplish in this meeting?* I knew that if I wanted to clear the air with Charles and get the team moving forward, I had to let go of my old assumptions. Everything depended on it.

"I'm all ears," I said.

"It's something Joseph showed us," Charles said. "He called it Q-Storming."

At that moment you could have knocked me over with a feather. Just a day before I would have done anything to shut Charles down. Today I just said, "Tell me about it."

Charles got up and went over to the flipchart that had become a permanent fixture in my office and picked up a blue felt-tip marker. "The goal," he explained, "is not to come up with answers, ideas, or suggestions. Instead we want to come up with as many new questions as possible. Just throw out questions as fast as we can, while I write them down."

"In other words, with no responses or discussion in between," I guessed.

"Exactly. Joseph said the goal is to open new doors in our minds...like behind every door we might find another answer or solution. Every new question just expands our range of possibilities. I think his exact words were, 'A question not asked is a door not opened.'"

> ## A question not asked
> ## is a door not opened.

"You always start by describing the problematic situation and your goals for change," Charles explained. "After that you figure out what assumptions you have about the situation."

"You mean like the assumption I made that you'd have trouble working with me," I said.

Charles cringed, but then nodded. "Once you've got your goals and assumptions clarified you start brainstorming new questions. For example, you might ask, *How can we work together to meet our targets?*" He wrote that question on the flipchart. After that, he immediately added another question: *What do I want to change about the team?*

"What *don't* we want to change!" I exclaimed.

"Joseph says the secret of successful Q-Storming is to stay in Learner and be careful about how you phrase the questions," Charles continued. "If we're to get the results we're seeking, the questions need to be in the first person...in other words, asking in terms of *I* or *we*."

"Okay," I said. "You mean like, *What would I like to see happen that isn't happening now? How can we all listen better? What can I do to be more creative?*"

"Great questions," Charles said, writing as fast as he could and underlining all the *I's* and *we's*.

I'm not sure where it came from but right after he said this, a new question popped out of my mouth: *"How can I keep the communication channels open between you and me and our other team members?"*

I thought I saw Charles smile, but he didn't say anything, just wrote my last question on the flipchart. Then he added another of his own: *How can I keep asking the right kinds of questions?*

"*How do we state our goals better, so everybody can be more aligned?*"

"*...and inspired?*" Charles added.

"Exactly," I said.

"Let's keep going. More questions!" Charles exclaimed.

He continued to jot them down on the flipchart, scrawling them out with the blue felt-tip pen.

"*What kind of fuel can I bring to keep our team running?*"

"*How do I keep from being judgmental?*"

"*How do I define responsibilities for each team member?*"

"*How do we make sure we all follow through on all our promises?*"

"*How can I assure each member it's okay to ask for help?*"

We both fired off questions in rapid succession. I was surprised at how naturally and easily Charles and I were working together. In no time we had four sheets covered with questions and they were all over the floor. Finally, I suggested we stop and review what we'd done.

Charles stepped back from the flipchart and said, "Joseph explained that it was important to notice if there are any questions we hadn't asked before. The new questions can make the biggest difference."

I quickly looked over the list still on the flipchart and shuffled through the sheets of questions on the floor. "Yes, quite a few," I admitted, frankly startled at how many I really hadn't asked.

Charles and I stood in front of the flipchart and then taped the other sheets up on the wall. We spent the next half hour looking over all our questions and adding new ones here and there. As we began discussing them I got clearer about why we'd been stuck and what would help us change.

Seeing all those questions written down helped me look at my present situation more objectively. Q-Storming allowed me to see possibilities beyond what I otherwise would have ever come up with. I remembered Alexa's story about her big breakthrough, how changing the kinds of questions she asked had changed the whole company. I was getting an inkling of how that could happen for us as well.

Charles was copying our questions into a notebook for later reference.

I perched on the edge of my desk, staring at the flip-chart. "I think I have a question to add to our list," I said. I went up to the chart, turned to a new sheet and wrote, *What will help each of us make our best contribution?*

"Nice," Charles said, nodding.

That word, *contribution*, suddenly became the central focus of my attention. In my zeal to assert my old role as the Answer Man, I had hardly ever asked questions such as, *What do other people have to offer? What do they need and want? What is my effect on them?* I saw even more deeply how the failure of the team — the team I used to call a night-mare — had been me. I had been the problem all along!

"I think I could spend the next few hours discussing what we've just accomplished here," I said. "But do you know what the most valuable lessons are for me in all of this?"

Charles shook his head.

"First, this was a great demonstration that questions have the power to open things up and maybe even turn things around. I can imagine using Q-Storming with the team—and as soon as possible! Second, I've got a whole new perspective on the ways that questions can help us better appreciate and understand the people around us."

These revelations were opening another very big door for me, with a new question coming into sharp focus: *Am I willing to allow others to contribute to me?*

"Ben," Charles said. "Before this meeting, I wasn't at all sure I would be able to stay on here at QTec. To tell the truth, working with you had started feeling like it was more trouble than it was worth."

"That painful, huh?" I felt my face break into an embarrassed grin, then I just laughed out loud. "I sympathize with you entirely," I said, warmly extending my hand to him. We had made our peace. In the process I'd made the breakthrough I'd been looking for—and changing my questions had been the pivot that made the difference. I could hardly wait to tell Joseph what had happened.

After Charles left my office, I went back to the flipchart and started blocking out plans for meeting with our team the following morning. This time I wanted to have the right questions to create a Learner environment. I sat down at my desk, pulled out my notes from my meetings with Joseph and began thumbing through them.

I leaned back in my chair and stared at the little placard on the wall: "Question everything!" Yes, I thought, Joseph was right. It all seemed so simple now. Right. Simple like Einstein's theory of relativity!

11 | *Amour! Amour!*

That night, charged up by all that happened in the meetings with Alexa and Charles, I worked late. In fact, I worked till long after dark, making notes for the meeting the next morning with Charles and the team. I also sent an email to Alexa to check on Joseph's availability for meeting with us within the next few weeks. Time raced by. When I remembered to check the clock it was two hours past the time I told Grace I'd be home. I considered calling but figured she'd be in bed sound asleep, so I decided not to disturb her. On the way home in the car I noticed it was going on eleven.

When I walked in the house I found Grace sitting alone in the dimly lit living room. She was in her pajamas, reading by a single lamp beside her chair. The moment I greeted her, I knew something was wrong. She silently set aside her book, walked up to me, took my hand, led me over to the sofa and told me, gently, to sit down. I sat, half expecting her to announce that someone had died — or that she was leaving me. She leaned forward in her chair, elbows on her knees, gazing into my eyes in a way that made it quite clear that this was going to be a serious talk.

"Ben," she said, "you have *got* to tell me what's going on with you."

Just as I'd done so many times before, my first instinct was to shrug it off. "I worked late. I told your secretary...and I considered calling but figured you were asleep."

"It's not about that. You know it isn't." She fixed me with a stare that told me she wasn't going to back off.

"There's been a lot of pressure at work...deadlines coming up way too fast...but I think there was some real progress today...." I knew I was waffling, but to tell the truth I was scared to death.

Grace shook her head slowly, paused, then asked, "What is it you need right now?"

For a moment I was speechless. Wasn't this the very question I'd asked myself about Charles? *What does the other person need and want?* Was she reading my mind, or had she somehow seen Joseph's *Top Twelve Questions for Success?*

"What do I need?" I echoed nervously. "You know, at this point I'm not even sure." I wasn't lying to her. I really didn't know.

"Here's what I've been noticing," Grace began. "Not long after you took this job, our whole relationship changed. You changed. I began to worry it was something about me. Did you suddenly feel that marrying me had been a mistake? Had I done something that offended or hurt you?"

I held up my hand. "Oh, Grace, it isn't anything like that!"

"That's what I realized after studying the Choice Map," she said. "You know what became clear — we've both been going down the Judger Path. I know I've been judging myself and you, and I see you being in Judger, too."

I had been bursting to tell her about my breakthrough with Charles, how it had already changed so much for me at work. But all I could say was that I agreed with her — and that I'd been looking carefully at how my being so Judger affected me and everyone around me.

"I'm filled with questions about us," Grace continued. "But until this afternoon my questions were mostly Judger ones. Then I started looking for things I might do or say to keep us from getting stuck in the Judger Pit."

"This is really hard for me to hear," I said, bowing my head, "I guess there's no easy way to say this...no other way through it..."

Grace suddenly looked as pale as a ghost. "Please let

this not be what I'm thinking," she said, her voice shaky and fearful.

"What?" An alarm went off in me. All sorts of possibilities raced through my mind. She huddled in her chair, staring at me. I took a deep breath. "Wait. What *are* you thinking? You don't think..."

"It's all the long nights you've spent at the office, all the excuses for not coming home, failing to call even to let me know where you were, not having time for me...for us." She paused. "Well?"

"Grace...I swear, it's nothing like that." This was an extremely difficult moment for me, for both of us. It had never occurred to me that she might have interpreted my long hours at work like this.

I shook my head slowly, partly because I couldn't believe what I was hearing, and partly to assure her I was not having an affair. "I would never do that, Grace." I gave a lot of thought to what I was going to say next. "There's something I want to tell you that I'm finding very difficult to say. I hope you won't end up hating me for it...maybe even as much as if there'd been another woman."

I guess I was getting a bit emotional at that moment. My face felt hot and my eyes were threatening to tear up. I had no idea what Grace's reaction would be in the next few moments. I was afraid that she might walk out on me when I told her the truth about my failures at work.

"I didn't exactly tell you the truth about Joseph and

how I got the Choice Map," I began. "As I saw it, I had to choose between going to him for executive coaching or handing in my resignation."

"Your resignation! Is that what this is all about? Oh, Ben, I'm so sorry!"

"For months now I was afraid I wasn't cut out to be a leader. Working with this team has been a real bust," I told her. "And if this job didn't work out…well, I was afraid of how it would affect you and me. Frankly, I was afraid you'd think I wasn't good enough for you."

We were both silent for several moments, then she asked quietly, "When did you first realize things weren't working out in the new job?"

"A few weeks into it," I confessed. "At first it was great. I really thought I could handle the team thing. Then I was hit with one challenge after another that I just couldn't manage, until I felt like I was drowning…"

"Wait," she interrupted. "You've had all of that going on for all this time and you never told me about it?"

"You're angry, Grace, aren't you? I just knew it was going to turn out like this. I'm really sorry. But I think things are turning around for me, in fact, I'm sure of it.…"

"Wait a second," Grace said. "Back up. You knew *what*? What did you think was going to turn out like this? Do you know why I'm angry at you? Are you sure you know why?"

"Of course I do. For screwing up at this job."

"No! No! No! That's not it at all!" She practically shouted this at me.

"Then for what?" I asked, totally taken aback. Had she found some offense that was even worse, something I didn't even know about yet? I wracked my brain for an explanation.

"What I'm upset about is that you've kept your problems a secret from me. You're my husband and you didn't let me know about something this important to *both* of us."

"I had every intention of telling you, but only after I got things rolling again. I was pretty sure I could get a new job right away, and things would get better and you would never have to know."

"In other words, you were going to continue covering this up and keeping me in the dark." Suddenly she looked like she wanted to punch me. "Good grief, Ben, how could you be so clueless?"

I stared back at her like she was a stranger. I really didn't know what to say.

"Listen to me," she said. "You better get what I'm about to say or we're never going to make it. I want you to share what's real with me, your troubles, your doubts, your victories, all of it. I *need* you to. That's such an important part of marriage for me. That's what helps me feel connected. When I'm having trouble at work, I talk it over with you, don't I?"

"Sure. I guess you do. I never thought about it much."

"Do you remember what I asked you when you came in tonight?"

"Yes, you asked me what I needed."

"You haven't yet answered me," she said. "I want you to. Right now."

My jaw dropped and I just stared into Grace's eyes for a long time. I don't know how much time passed. Maybe it was just seconds, but those moments are imprinted in my mind forever. *What do you need?* Those four words, said with so much loving care, were like laser beams cutting through a stone wall for me.

"What I want..." I began, "I guess if I'm being totally honest right now, I want to tell you everything that's been happening to me and not let my fears stop me."

I paused to check out Grace's expression before continuing. She was smiling but there was something else in her face that I couldn't quite read. In spite of that, I had to press on.

"I've had to confront my own limitations," I began, working up my courage. "I've spent way too much time in Judger and have made a lot of assumptions — hurtful ones — about myself as well as other people. All of this has caused major problems at work. And one of the toughest parts I've had to face is that... well, there's more to life than being the Answer Man. I've got a huge amount to learn. At least now I've got some better choices, thanks to our friend Joseph."

At that point, I poured out the whole story of what I'd gone through the past few months, how I'd been scared to death that if I didn't succeed in this new position, Alexa would conclude that I couldn't make it at QTec. There had been so many days I felt like a loser that I didn't dare admit I was sliding faster and faster into the Judger Pit. When I got to the end of my story, Grace came over and sat close to me and draped her arms around me.

"I love you very much," she said. "I love you even more because of all that you've just shared with me. But promise me that you'll never hold out on me again. Promise?"

"It's not going to be easy," I told her. "Habits are hard to break. Besides, at work I've learned that you don't get ahead by whining."

"You're not whining! There's a huge difference between being a crybaby and being honest. We should always be open to asking each other what's going on and feel safe about telling the truth. Let's remember we're in this together."

There it was again...creating the room for people to ask questions openly and contribute to each other. This conversation was taking the breakthrough I'd had at work to a whole new level. Did I fully understand it all yet? I didn't. But what I did see, quite clearly, was that Joseph's methods worked as well at home as they did at work.

I don't remember the exact words I used though I do remember telling Grace how much this breakthrough with her meant to me. I thanked her for asking the questions she had, for listening to my problems, and for patiently working together through a very difficult time.

I felt Grace's arms around me. She kissed me gently on the lips. In that instant, I knew something important had changed, not just between Grace and me but in the whole way I looked at the world.

As we headed for the stairs that night, our arms were still around each other, making it difficult to walk. We laughed as we stumbled comically on the first steps. I told her we'd never make it to the top entwined like this.

She smiled playfully: "But we could try."

We kissed again and I suddenly got serious: "Can I ask you a question?"

"Anytime," Grace said, with a sparkle in her eyes. "Just anytime at all."

12   *The Inquiring Leader*

Sitting behind my desk this afternoon, I'm remembering that terrible day when I drafted my resignation letter from QTec. Months after that, when I was pretty sure I'd turned things around and was out of the woods, I got a call that unnerved me. My secretary buzzed and said that Alexa wanted me in her office right away — and "Bring that green folder with you" — I'd know what she was talking about. That sounded pretty ominous because the folder she described was the one that contained my resignation.

I dropped what I was doing, grabbed the folder, and

started down the hall. Just as I raised my hand to knock on the big double doors of Alexa's office, I heard voices inside, which made me even more concerned. Rattled by memories of that earlier visit, when I'd come with resignation in hand, my Judger started clamoring for attention. I steadied myself, took a deep breath, stepped into Learner, and tapped lightly on the door.

Seconds later, Alexa was greeting me with a friendly smile. As I stepped across the threshold I saw Joseph inside, sitting in the meeting area on one of the two sofas. As I approached he stood up and we shook hands warmly. I began to relax a little but still couldn't make sense of the situation.

As I did my best to make myself comfortable on the sofa opposite Joseph, I noticed what might be a framed picture turned face down on the wide coffee table between us. Alexa pointed to the folder in my lap and asked, "Did you bring the envelope?" I must have looked puzzled for she then added, "Don't you remember? Months ago, you came to see me ready to resign. After we talked and you agreed to see Joseph, I gave you an envelope with a prediction inside. You put it in that green folder. It's time for you to open it."

Then it came back to me. I opened the folder, took out the still sealed envelope, and tore it open. The note inside, hastily written in Alexa's hand, said simply: "Ben in Joseph's Hall of Fame."

I looked from Alexa to Joseph, searching for some clue

about what this all meant. Then Joseph picked up the frame I'd noticed on the coffee table, turned it over and handed it to me. The first thing I saw was my own photo at the top of a certificate.

"Ben, when I hired you I knew it was a gamble even though you're technically the best in the business. But you'd never held a leadership position before. On the other hand, I'd also never seen you face a challenge that you didn't eventually master. After you agreed to work with Joseph, I predicted that you would not only rise to the occasion but also make it into his Question Thinking Hall of Fame," Alexa explained. "And happily you've proved me right."

Joseph smiled broadly as I began reading the text on the certificate. It described how my progress using Question Thinking had qualified me for his Hall of Fame. It told how I had changed my old question — *How can I prove I'm right?* — into ones that made all the difference for me and my team. My new questions were true Learner ones: *How can I understand?* And *What are others thinking, feeling, and wanting?* As simple as this now looked on paper, it had been a huge breakthrough for me, changing how I approached problems but more importantly how I valued and worked with the people around me.

Those new questions had led to still others: *How can I allow other people to contribute to me?* And, *How can I contribute to others?* Once I realized I didn't have to have all the answers, everything went easier. People shared their ideas, asked lots more questions, and really listened to each other. I thought about something Joseph had once quoted to me: "Words create worlds." I had learned through my own experience how literally true that was. My new Question Thinking skills had helped to transform us into a high-performing Learner team.

Words create worlds.

The other major thing Joseph noted on the certificate was how well Charles and I had worked together to bring Q-Storming to our team. The new questions we discovered through Q-Storming led to the breakthrough we needed to get our product to market ahead of our competition. After that, QTec had established a solid and consistent upward trajectory that otherwise might have never been possible.

Less than a year after that milestone meeting with Alexa and Joseph, Alexa came to my office holding the printout of an email she'd just received from the *Wall Street Journal* that she wanted to share with me. It was the advance copy of an article they would publish in a few days. It described our successful turnaround and attributed our triumph to what the writer called "the culture of inquiring leadership that characterizes QTec." Alexa had highlighted two places where my name was mentioned.

If there was ever a day to celebrate, that was it! But

celebrating would have to wait. As I recall, all this happened only hours before Alexa was to leave for a conference in Washington, D.C. She was going to deliver a keynote titled *The Inquiring Leader: The Leadership We Need for the 21st Century.*

When she returned from Washington, Alexa called a special meeting with Joseph and me. She began by sharing her experience of that conference. "I was very encouraged by what I heard there," she explained. "Leaders everywhere have a growing appreciation for the power of questions to help people become more creative and collaborative, not to mention more productive and profitable.

"On the way home, I had the realization that it's time to more systematically drive Question Thinking through our whole organization. While we've obviously made some great changes, *sustained* change that is positive requires shared practices that get integrated into everyone's behavior everyday."

Then Alexa looked me straight in the eye and I knew she wanted my full attention. "I'm moving Charles into your position," she said. "He's been ready for a while."

For an instant I found myself wobbling toward the Judger Path. The suggestion that Charles would replace me brought up some of those old negative feelings about him. My Judger reaction startled me and I quickly put it to rest.

"I'd like you to coach Charles through the transition," Alexa continued. "As for you, Ben, you're getting *two* promotions. While it's true you got a shaky start here at QTec, with Joseph's coaching you've turned into a real leader. And your team proved it when they hit one out of the park on that first product. Now I believe you can take us to the next level with some products that are even more technically challenging — and more promising."

Before I could even catch my breath from my excited reaction to Alexa's announcement, she hit me with the next one.

"Second, I want you to head up the leadership team that will bring Question Thinking to QTec from top to bottom. I want everyone in the company to know these tools, use them, and reap the benefits, for the further success of the company as well as for themselves.

"Joseph will work closely with you and this team. He and I are both convinced that this will make us a model Learner organization."

I swallowed hard and said, "This is great news, but are you sure I'm the right guy? Nobody resisted Joseph's teachings more than I did. This didn't come easily for me, as you know."

Joseph smiled. "That's what makes you perfect," he said. "As I told Alexa last week, she needs someone who knows all the arguments for not adopting Question Thinking. She needs a person who knows what it is to resist with all his might...."

"And have his life changed by it," I added easily. What

leapt into my mind wasn't work at all but the wonderful time I had had with Grace the night before. Our relationship had grown in amazing ways since my first breakthroughs with Question Thinking. We now had the kind of marriage I'd only dreamt might be possible. Sometimes Grace even teases me that we have an *inquiring marriage*.

"Any questions?" Alexa asked.

"Questions?" I responded. "Oh, you bet, a million of them! I've become a champion of that Einstein quote you've got posted all over the place — *Question everything!*"

Joseph nodded, and then suddenly burst out laughing. "You two are an amazing pair," he said. "Great things are happening around here, for everybody. Given how much has already been accomplished leads me to wonder, *What further possibilities can we discover together?*"

> ## Great results begin with great questions!

Question Thinking: 10 Powerful Tools for Life and Work

In these pages, you'll find the ten Question Thinking tools that Joseph introduced to Ben, in approximately the same order as they occur in the story. I've also included page references so you can refer back to see how Ben applied and benefited from each one. Each tool is an integral facet of the Question Thinking system, so you may notice that they overlap as well as complement one another. Most importantly, just as in developing any new skill, the more you use these tools, the more proficient you will become.

Many companies use the book, including the

material in this Tools Section, as the basis for discussion groups focused on team collaboration, productivity, and innovation. Many also post copies of the Choice Map in their offices and meeting rooms. Another possibility is to use these tools to supplement some of the QT web-based learning offered by the Inquiry Institute.

As you learned through the story, QTec also make a positive difference for people in their personal lives, including with concerns about relationships, finances, health, and weight. Self-help groups, book clubs, and church groups actively use the ideas and principles in *Change Your Questions, Change Your Life* for study and guidance.

I'd love to hear from you. It would be especially great to receive stories about how Question Thinking has made a difference anywhere in your life — at work and at home.

The 10 Tools of Question Thinking

Tool 1.   Empower Your Observer

Tool 2.   Use the Choice Map as a Guide

Tool 3.   Put the Power of Questions to Work

Tool 4.   Distinguish Learner and Judger Mindsets
and Questions

Tool 5.   Make Friends with Judger

Tool 6.   Question Assumptions

Tool 7.   Take Advantage of Switching Questions

Tool 8.   Create Learner Teams

Tool 9.   Create Breakthroughs with Q-Storming®

Tool 10. Ask the Top Twelve Questions for Success

Tool 1: Empower Your Observer

See Chapter 2, "A Challenge Accepted," pages 19–34.

Purpose: To develop the ability to be still, calm, and present with ourselves and others. This capacity is the foundation of equanimity that helps us become more centered, resourceful, and strategic.

Discussion: In Chapter 2, Ben begins learning how to stand outside himself and nonjudgmentally witness his thoughts, feelings, and actions. Joseph explains that we all have this observer capacity. It is sometimes experienced as a feeling of watching a movie in which we are one of the actors. The more we develop our observer capacity, the more in charge we can be of our thoughts, feelings, and actions — and the less we can be controlled by people and events outside ourselves.

From the position of observer, we have the ability to simply notice *what is*, somewhat detached from our own thoughts and feelings. We become more able to distinguish between our own sense of what's true and what's actually happening around us. It is a way of being more "mindful" of the role our own emotions, opinions, or attachments play in how we view the world. Many spiritual and philosophical traditions recognize this observer capacity as a natural ability that is strengthened by practices such as meditation and the ones described in this section.

Is it ever possible to become 100 percent objective and open to what's true and real? Probably not. But switching into observer mode, to any degree, is an invaluable skill for negotiating change, making decisions, operating effectively under pressure, and relating well to others. From the observer self we are in an ideal position to recognize the kinds of questions we're asking and switch to Learner when we find ourselves on the Judger Path.

Here are three simple ways to start empowering your observer capacity.

Practice 1: The next time your phone rings, at home or at work, stay still and just let it ring. In fact, listen to the ringing. As you do, observe your reaction to the ringing, such as your desire to act by rushing to the phone and picking it up. Carefully observe what's going through your mind and body, without taking action (i.e., answering the phone) or becoming attached to the thoughts and feelings that are triggered by the ringing phone.

If you wish, imagine that your thoughts and feelings are like clouds moving across the sky and you're simply and calmly watching the shifting picture.

Practice 2: When you get into a challenging situation where you have an impulse to act, or you have thoughts or feelings you want to express, just step into your observer mode. Remind yourself that, just as with the ringing phone, you do not have to "answer" those impulses. You can learn to simply watch. Then, when you do take action, you will be more thoughtful, strategic, and mindful of potential outcomes.

Practice 3: The next time you're faced with an important choice, or when you notice you've been hijacked by Judger, take a few quiet minutes to be alone. Sit quietly, noting whatever you are thinking, feeling, or wanting at that moment. Promise yourself that regardless of what you observe, this is not yet a time for action. Simply observe and note.

In the most expansive sense, the observer is calmly asking a single Self-Q: *What's present now?* moment by moment by moment. As your observer becomes more robust and effective, you will become better and better at recognizing when you're in Judger, and simply accepting that this is momentarily the way it is. It is this moment of "wake-up," noting where you are, that grants each of us the liberating power of true choice.

Tool 2: Use the Choice Map as a Guide

See Chapter 3, "The Choice Map," pages 35–52.

Purpose: To provide a visual summary and guide for understanding our Learner/Judger mindsets and questions and the future that these create.

Discussion: Throughout Ben's story, the Choice Map helps him become aware of the kinds of questions he's asking — Learner or Judger — and consider how he might change his questions for the best results. Here are four ways to work with the Choice Map.

Practice 1: Imagine that you are the figure standing at the crossroads of the Choice Map. Some thought, feeling, or circumstance has just occurred. It might be related to your business, career, or personal life. Experiment by taking each path separately, i.e., asking yourself both Judger and Learner questions about this situation and carefully considering the results each might produce. If you land in Judger, consider what Switching question might allow you to step onto the Switching Lane and return to Learner territory. Looking at the Choice Map, you can simply ask: *Where am I right now? Am I in Judger? Where do I want to be? What is my ultimate goal in this situation?*

Practice 2: You can use the Choice Map to learn from a past situation that didn't work out as you would have liked. It can help you discover if a Judger hijacking might have blocked your success. If so, what lessons can you learn from this? How would you handle that same situation now, using your Learner mindset?

Practice 3: You can also use the Choice Map to learn from a situation that *did* work. What Learner questions made the difference? How did those questions help you avoid the Judger Pit? If any Judger was present, what Switching questions did you use to move onto the Learner Path? What lessons can you draw from these observations that you might want to reinforce and benefit from again in the future?

Practice 4: Share the Choice Map with others, at work and at home, and you'll gain at least as much as you give. There's an old medical school saying: "See one, do one, teach one, and it's yours!" You could, for example, share it with a team, project group, or coachee. Many readers also share the Choice Map with family members and friends. This is an ideal way to reinforce Learner relationships and results with people anywhere in your life. Make sure you're in Learner when you share the Choice Map with others!

Tool 3: Put the Power of Questions to Work

See Chapter 2, "A Challenge Accepted," pages 19–34.

This tool has two parts: The first (A) has to do with becoming more prolific and effective at asking Internal Questions (the ones we ask ourselves); the second (B) has to do with becoming more prolific and effective at asking Interpersonal Questions (those we ask others).

A: Internal Questions

Purpose: To become more aware of your Self-Q's and to increase the quantity and quality of your internal questions.

Discussion: Ben starts to change once he realizes that the questions he asks himself—both Learner and Judger—have a huge impact on the results he's able to achieve. He then begins refining his questions by applying the tools in the Question Thinking system.

All our actions are driven by internal questions that we may or may not be aware of asking ourselves. Even an ordinary activity such as getting ready to go on a family vacation is driven by questions. For example, think of a time when you were packing for a trip. You went to your closet, your bureau, and your medicine cabinet and asked yourself questions such as: *What climate(s) will we be in? Do I need evening as well as casual clothes? What packs well and doesn't wrinkle?* And *How long will we be gone?* You answered your questions first in your mind and then by *doing* something. You selected some items and put them in your suitcase.

As you think about packing for travel, notice that you would ask yourself very different questions depending on whether you were going, say, on an African safari or a lovely week in Paris. And what if you arrived at your destination and discovered you'd forgotten something? That just means you forgot to ask yourself about that item, either when you were planning or packing for your trip.

These two practices for increasing your awareness of Self-Q's are very simple. The first turns your attention to how *prevalent* questions are in your life. The second focuses on the questions and statements in our thinking and the kinds of results they produce.

Practice 1: When you get up tomorrow morning, do a little question research. Note what questions you're asking yourself as you get dressed. Then, from time to time throughout the day, ask yourself what questions might be driving your behavior in the situation, both in terms of your own actions and your interactions with others. It may take some patient observing to recognize those behavior-generating questions, but stay with it until you are able to see the influential role that Self-Q's play in your life.

Practice 2: As a second piece of question research, notice your responses to situations that come up throughout the day. Is your first thought a statement (an answer), or is it a question? If your first thought is a statement, experiment with changing it into a question; notice how shifting from a statement to a question changes your moods, actions, or interactions. Notice any correlations between your statements or questions and the kinds of results they produce.

B: Interpersonal Questions

Purpose: To become more aware of the questions you ask other people, including the impact of your questions on them, and to increase the quantity and quality of your interpersonal questions.

Discussion: Throughout Ben's story, Joseph helps him to understand the importance of asking questions to:
- Gather information
- Create understanding and learning
- Build, improve, and sustain relationships
- Clarify and confirm listening
- Stimulate creativity and innovation
- Resolve conflicts
- Create collaboration
- Set goals and create action plans
- Explore, discover, and create new possibilities

Practice 1: Approximately what is the ratio of questions you ask versus statements you make (your ask/tell ratio)? Do your communications with others involve more questions and fewer statements or answers? In at least one conversation today, practice asking *many* questions.

Practice 2: Recall a time when a particular question made a positive difference in your personal or professional life. What was the question? What was the result? And what was it about the question that made such a difference?

Tool 4. Distinguish Learner and Judger Mindsets and Questions

See Chapter 3, "The Choice Map," page 50
for the list of Learner and Judger Questions.

See Chapter 6, "Switching Questions," page 86
for the full Learner/Judger Chart.

Purpose: To help you distinguish between Learner and Judger mindsets and how they affect your thinking, actions, relationships, and results.

Discussion: In Chapter 3, Joseph shows Ben how to use the list of Learner/Judger Questions to identify the kinds of questions he's asking and their impact on him, on other people, and on situations around him. As Ben gains greater facility with Question Thinking, Joseph gives him tools to identify Learner and Judger mindsets and relationships.

The following exercise allows you to have an experience similar to Ben's as he refines his ability to recognize intellectual, emotional, and physical differences between being in Learner and being in Judger.

Practice: Look at the Judger column of the Learner/Judger Questions and notice how the questions affect you physically, emotionally, and intellectually. If you're like most people, Judger questions may lead you to feel de-energized, fearful, negative, tense, or even a little "blue." I often do this exercise in workshops. Some people have reported that they held their breath or even got a headache from thinking the Judger questions!

Now it's time to switch to Learner. Take a deep breath, let go of Judger, and then slowly read the Learner questions on the right side of the chart. Notice how you feel now. Many people report that Learner questions make them feel energized, optimistic, open, hopeful, and more relaxed. They feel encouraged to look for solutions and possibilities. As one man noted, "When I'm looking with Learner eyes, I feel hopeful about the future."

You may discover, as Ben did, how questions associated with these two mindsets put you in distinctly different moods — and that these different moods position you to act and relate quite differently. You may also discover that the world of experience and possibility is different in Learner than it is in Judger.

Explore how one or the other mindset impacts how you interact with the people around you. How does Judger mindset — yours or theirs — affect communications with a co-worker, spouse, child, or friend? Then ask yourself about the impact of Learner mindset.

Tool 5. Make Friends with Judger

See Chapter 4, "We're All Recovering Judgers," pages 53–62.

Purpose: To become more aware and accepting of Judger mindset in ourselves and others.

Discussion: In Chapter 4, Ben's growing awareness of his Judger mindset causes him to get increasingly frustrated with himself. But Joseph helps him to move beyond this seeming double bind by encouraging him to make friends with Judger.

The more accepting and friendly we can be toward Judger—in ourselves and others—the more liberated we become to make the best choices in any situation. Our awareness and acceptance of Judger is important because it strengthens our ability to switch to Learner. It is in Learner that we are most resourceful, strategic, and connected with others.

Engaging in each of the following practices will heighten your awareness of Judger. After you complete each one, write down your observations, reflections, and appreciations for the information and freedom that recognizing and accepting Judger provides for you.

Practice 1: Keep a journal and jot down times when you catch yourself and others in Judger. Include any actual Judger questions you notice yourself asking. You might also include any physical sensations or moods you associate with Judger.

Practice 2: Place a rubber band around your wrist and snap it lightly any time you notice you've been hijacked by Judger. Then, each time you snap the rubber band, congratulate yourself for your increasing awareness of Judger!

Practice 3: Allot a ten-minute period in some neutral situation, such as watching TV, to purposefully be as Judger as you possibly can be. For example, you might be openly judgmental or critical of a newscaster's hair style, voice quality, or clothing. This will heighten your awareness of Judger and also your ability to move out of that mindset.

Practice 4: Recognize that every time you do these practices you reinforce your observer self and your ability to operate from Learner. This is one of the many benefits we accrue simply by noticing and accepting Judger!

Practice 5: Don't go Judger on your Judger!

Tool 6. Question Assumptions

See Chapter 9, "When the Magic Works," pages 113–126.

Purpose: To avoid making mistakes and suffering unintended consequences based on false or incomplete information.

Discussion: You may remember that both Ben and Grace make faulty assumptions about co-workers. And these faulty assumptions undermine effective communication, making it impossible to build or maintain satisfying relationships.

To make an assumption is to believe that something is true without necessarily any basis in fact. False assumptions can sabotage our efforts to achieve our goals and deepest desires. Once we are able to bring any blind spots in our assumptions to light, we gain new insights and creative possibilities that allow us to move forward in more positive ways.

How do you detect the accuracy of your own assumptions so they don't trip you up? First is the courage and willingness to discover them. The habit of asking skillful questions, both of ourselves and others, is our best tool for uncovering blind spots and moving beyond them to discover valuable new information, perspectives, and possibilities.

Practice: Think of a situation in which you are stuck, frustrated, or where you want a change. Use the following list of assumption-busting questions to help you take a disciplined approach to unearth any false or faulty assumptions that might be blocking your success. For best results, consider each question thoroughly and write down your responses. Often, the act of writing stimulates deeper reflection and discoveries.

+ What assumptions am I making about myself?
+ What assumptions am I making about others?
+ What am I assuming from the past that may not be true now?
+ What am I assuming about available resources?
+ What am I assuming about what's impossible — or possible?

Tool 7. Take Advantage of Switching Questions

See Chapter 6, "Switching Questions," pages 73–90.

For the ABCC formula, see Chapter 7, "Seeing with New Eyes, Hearing with New Ears," pages 91–98.

Purpose: To facilitate easier course corrections from the Judger Path onto the Learner Path.

Discussion: In Chapter 6, Joseph introduces Switching questions, a special kind of Learner question that depends first on being able to observe Judger. Ben learns to ask Switching questions whenever he finds himself in Judger. The Choice Map helps him remember this shortcut from Judger back to Learner.

Think of Switching questions as "rescue," "turnaround," or "course correction" questions. They can literally *rescue* you from Judger consequences. Switching questions can give you not only the opportunity to choose a new course, but sometimes to make major breakthroughs. Just as with developing any other new ability, the more you use Switching questions the better you get at it and the more natural it feels.

By their very nature, Switching questions are *from-to* questions, meaning they can carry us *from* Judger *to* Learner. We all use Switching questions whether we realize it or not; the more aware we are of how they work, the more we are able to employ them on purpose.

The best Switching questions are those that feel most natural and accessible to you. These are the questions you most easily and consistently reach for and use. The more *grooved in* they are, the more effective they will be. The following list of Switching questions includes some contributed by participants in workshops over the years.

Am I in Judger?
Is this what I want to feel?
Is this what I want to be doing?
Where would I rather be?
How can I get there?
Is this working?
What are the facts?
How *else* can I think about this?
What assumptions am I making?
What am I missing or avoiding?
How can I be more objective and honest?
What is the other person thinking, feeling,
    and wanting?
What's surprising?
Is this the hill I want to die on?
What humor can I find in this situation?
What's my choice right now?

This is an evolving, growing list, and I encourage you to customize it by adding your own Switching questions.

Practice 1: Think of past situations that were difficult or frustrating for you but which you managed to turn around. Think about what your Switching questions might have been in those situations. Why did they make a difference? When you discover the questions you asked intuitively, you'll be able to use them more intentionally, skillfully, and quickly.

Practice 2: The ABCC Choice Process. Pick a challenging situation in which you desire a change and follow the ABCC format described in Ben's story in Chapter 7.

Tool 8. Create Learner Teams

See Chapter 8, "Learner Teams and Judger Teams," pages 99–111.

Purpose: To learn about the benefits of applying Question Thinking and the Learner/Judger distinctions to teams as well as to organizations

Discussion: In Chapter 8, Joseph uses the Choice Map to explain the difference between Learner teams and Judger teams. Ben realizes that Learner teams are far more effective than Judger ones are. He begins to consider ways of turning his Judger team into a Learner team.

The experience of working on teams can be challenging and people often deal with these difficulties in Judger ways. They might stop listening, try to push their own agenda, or just blame others when things don't work out. They could go Judger on *themselves* by assuming they have nothing to contribute, by shutting down, and/or by not fully engaging. Whatever the case, nobody wins. By introducing the notion of Learner teams, each participant can follow guidelines to suspend Judger and simply step into Learner, which has a positive effect on everyone's productivity and results.

Practice 1: Ask people to compare their experiences of Learner teams versus Judger teams. You can also ask people to think of times they've been on teams that have worked well, when they've been able to contribute their best strengths to the task at hand — and teams when they haven't. Then simply ask them to describe the differences in terms of experience, productivity, and results.

Practice 2: Print out copies of the Choice Map (free color copies are available at www.InquiryInstitute.com) and give one to each team member. Lead a discussion about the impact of Learner and Judger mindsets for the team. Include the notions of Judger costs and Judger stand-off in your conversation. Then introduce the importance of a *Learner Alliance* (see pp. 107–108) and discuss what it would take for your team commit to creating a Learner Alliance.

Practice 3: Ask people on your team to generate guidelines based on the Choice Map about how to best communicate and collaborate during meetings.

Tool 9. Create Breakthroughs with Q-Storming®

See Chapter 10, "Q-Storming to the Rescue" pages 127–138.

Purpose: To facilitate collaborative, creative, and strategic thinking that can lead to more successful results.

Discussion: Joseph introduces the term Q-Storming to Ben and suggests that he ask Alexa about it, since she's used this practice so effectively. Ben learns how to do Q-Storming from Charles, and it contributes to a breakthrough for Ben and his eventual success.

Q-Storming is most often used when breakthroughs are sought in decision making, problem solving, strategic planning, and innovation. It is a tool for moving beyond limitations in perception and thinking and advancing to novel and extraordinary solutions and answers. While Q-Storming is akin to brainstorming, the goal of this Question Thinking practice is to generate as many questions as possible. The expectation is that some of these questions will provide desired new openings or directions. Typically, questions open thinking, while answers often close thinking.

Q-Storming is based on three premises: (1) Great results *begin* with great questions; (2) Most any problem can be solved with enough of the right *questions*; and (3) The questions we ask *ourselves* often provide the most fruitful openings for new thinking and possibilities.

Q-Storming is typically done with a group or team, especially when exploring ideas and possibilities. It is also used in goal-oriented conversations between two people, for example, in coaching, leadership, management, or sales. Q-Storming can be done in person or *virtually*, say with a global team or a coaching client in a different geographic location.

The facilitator focuses on developing a robust goal and eliciting assumptions about it prior to the question-generation phase of Q-Storming. Often at the end, action plans will be made or revised based on discoveries made during the Q-Storming session.

Question Guidelines

Questions should be first person singular or plural, using "I" and "we." You want new questions to *think with*, not necessarily to ask someone else.

Generate questions from Learner mindset and avoid Judger.

Questions are mostly open-ended, not closed ("How can I?" rather than "Can I?" and "How can we?" rather than "Can you?")

Invite courageous and provocative, as well as "silly" and "dumb" questions.

Note: Q-Storming is a powerful tool for creative thinking, and you are welcome to experiment with it. However, mastery with facilitating Q-Storming sessions — especially with groups or communities facing complex or challenging issues — is best supported by professional training. You can find more information about Q-Storming and Q-Storming training programs at www.InquiryInstitute.com.

Tool 10: Ask the Top Twelve Questions for Success

See Chapter 9, "When the Magic Works," pages 113–126.

Purpose: To offer a useful sequence of questions for thinking comprehensively before making a change or embarking on a new direction.

Discussion: Ben is caught in traffic and distressed about his upcoming meetings with Alexa and Charles. He calls Joseph, who gives him three of the Top Twelve Questions for Success. Those three questions help launch Ben into the series of breakthroughs that lead to his being able to apply Question Thinking for greater success and satisfaction in his life and work

The questions on the *Top Twelve List* evolved out of my work with coaching clients and workshop participants over many years. The list can be used in at least three ways: First, it is a logical sequence of questions to help you work through any situation you might want to change or improve. Second, you might just want to scan the list for questions you're missing in a particular situation. Third, you can turn to it when you're looking for just the right question to emphasize in a particular situation.

Within this list are questions that are applicable to a variety of life's challenges. The goal is to integrate these questions into your everyday thinking. Then, when a challenge arises, you'll be able to easily recall some of them. Not every question applies to every situation. That's why you'll want to develop a collection of your favorites and work with them on a regular basis. These questions can open and change your mind. They allow you to unveil new choices, options, and possibilities you might otherwise have missed.

Practice: Think of a situation in which you are stuck, frustrated, or want something to change. Within that situation, you can ask the questions on the list below from several perspectives. Ask them of yourself— *What do **I** want?* Ask them of other people — *What do **you** want?* Or ask them of those with whom you have an ongoing relationship — *What do **we** want?* Here's the list:

1. What do I want?
2. What are my choices?
3. What assumptions am I making?
4. What am I responsible for?
5. How else can I think about this?
6. What is the other person thinking, feeling, and wanting?
7. What am I missing or avoiding?
8. What can I learn?
   ...from this person or situation?
   ...from this mistake or failure?
   ...from this success?

9. What action steps make the most sense?
10. What questions should I ask (myself or others)?
11. How can I turn this into a win-win?
12. What's possible?

Keep this list in a handy place where you can refer to it often. If you ask these questions frequently enough, they'll become a natural part of your thinking. They'll help you create more satisfying and successful results in your life every day!

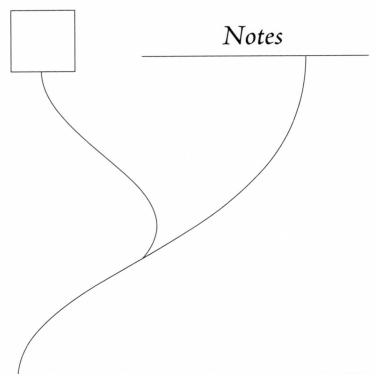

Notes

Page 2: "included in an article..." David Wolfskehl is the reader of the first edition whose successful application of the principles of Question Thinking was described in *Inc. Magazine*. See Leigh Buchanan, "In Praise of Selflessness," *Inc. Magazine* (May 2007).

Page 7: "*Change Your Questions* has struck a chord" My professional text, *The Art of the Question: A Guide to Short-Term Question-Centered Therapy*, was published by John Wiley & Sons in 1998. My maiden name was Marilee Goldberg.

Page 26: "nomadic societies were driven..." The example of questions that drove the behavior of nomads was ascribed to psychologist Mark Brown by Michael J. Gelb in *How to Think Like Leonardo da Vinci: Seven Steps to Genius Every Day* (Dell Publications, 2004).

Page 76: "'...the last of human freedoms—" This quote is from *Man's Search for Meaning* by Viktor E. Frankl (Beacon Press, 2006). Originally published in Austria in 1946 as *Ein Psychologe erlebt das Konzentrationslager* (which translates as "Saying yes to life in spite of everything; A psychologist experiences the concentration camp"). The English translation was first published by Beacon Press in 1959.

Pages 100–101: Joseph Campbell's story of the farmer and the quote, "Where you stumble, there your treasure is," comes from *An Open Life: Joseph Campbell in Conversation with Michael Toms*, selected and edited by John M. Maher and Dennie Briggs (Perennial Library, 1990).

Page 107: "high-performing teams consistently had a good balance between inquiry and advocacy..." This article describes research on the relationship between advocacy and inquiry on team performance. Frederickson L. Barbara and Marcial F. Losada, "Positive Affect and the Complex Dynamics of Human Flourishing," *The American Psychologist* (October 2005), 678-686.

Page 123: "two comparable bowling teams" The example about the effect on bowling teams of viewing videos of their successful moves in contrast to their mistakes is from: Kirschenbaum, D. "Self Regulation & Sport Psychology: Nurturing an Emerging Symbiosis." *Journal of Sport Psychology*, 1984, 8, 26-34.

Page 152: The concept that "words create worlds" relates to the Constructionist Principle of Appreciative Inquiry. See David L. Cooperrider, Frank Barrett, and Suresh Srivastva, "Social Construction and Appreciative Inquiry: A Journey in Organizational Theory," in *Management and Organization: Relational Alternatives to Individualism*, edited by Dian-Marie Hosking, H. Peter Dachler, and Kenneth J. Gergen (Avebury, 1995).

Acknowledgments

Writing the second edition of *Change Your Questions, Change Your Life* has been a rich and gratifying journey. My answers to the question, "To whom am I grateful?" are extensive and heartfelt.

Hal Zina Bennett again brought his wealth of wisdom, experience, and generosity to our writing partnership and friendship. His expert skills helped animate the spirit of inquiry in Question Thinking. To someone who is a wordsmith, my appreciation is beyond words.

The Inquiry Institute home team has provided an invaluable foundation of friendship and support. Kim Aubry has been the cornerstone. I am most grateful to her as well as to Peter Felperin, David Fisher, Sonia Helgesson, Amy Lenzo, Gaen Murphree, Debbie Tester Sakagawa, Melinda Sinclair, Carla Van Dyk, and T. Waldmann-Williams. I again thank Diane Chew for the title.

Berrett-Koehler exemplifies "publisher as partner," and all BK authors and our readers are the beneficiaries. Led by their visionary founder and publisher, Steve Piersanti, I am especially grateful to María Jesús Aguiló, Marina Cook, Michael Crowley, Kristen Franz, Catherine Lengronne, David Marshall, Dianne Platner, Jeevan Sivasubramaniam, Katie Sheehan, Jeremy Sullivan, Mark von Bronkhorst, Johanna Vondeling, and Rick Wilson.

I am delighted that a chance meeting with Cat Russo of the American Society of Training and Development (ASTD) led to their co-publishing this Second Edition. Also at ASTD, Mark Morrow, Jennifer Naughton, and Dean Smith have become valued partners.

Each of these—friends, family, and colleagues—has also contributed generously to me and my work: Rose Adams, Mark Annett, Beth Armbruster, Dick Axelrod, Emily Axelrod, Dawn Baron, Joan Barth, Ilene Becker, Larry Becker, Yury Boshyk, Pat Brewer, Juanita Brown, Lillian Brown, Tracey Pilkerton Cairnie, David Cooperrider, Elizabeth Corley, Lex Dilworth, Denise Easton, Marnie Escaf, Marilyn Figlar, Joan Geller, Pilar Gerasimo, Nick Gimbel, Phyllis Giovinco, LeRoy Goldberg, Selma Crockin

Goldberg, Pat Goldring, Grant Grayson, George Gross, Kathleen Higgins, Hallock Hoffman, Rebel Holiday, Lynne Hornyak, Susan Horowitz, David Isaacs, Larina Kase, Florence Kaslow, Sam Kirschner, Greg Kusic, Danielle LaPorte, Stewart Levine, Mark Levy, Shoshanna Liebman, Sharon Lockhart, Kate Marshall, Victoria Marsick, Mireille Massue, Petrina McGrath, Marsha George McLean, Hyman Meyers, Mark Miani, Kelle Olwyler, Linda J. Page, Michelle Pante, Detta Penna, Roy Plummer, Brad Pressman, Valerie Price, Don Proffit, Mary Beth Rebstock, Audrey Reed, Hildy Richelson, Stan Richelson, Myron Rogers, Sandy Roth, Cynda Rushton, Lee Salmon, Marge Schiller, Kitty Schwarzschild, Ron Sherman, Barbara Sloan, Mavis Smith, Therese Stanton, Diana Whitney, Gail Williams, Lou Wolfe, Sam Wurtzel, Andrea Zintz.

These colleagues, who are at the core of our learning community, the Learner Alliance, have dedicated themselves to becoming Question Thinkers. They've participated extensively in the Inquiry Institute's trainings and certification programs: Anne Albertine, Kim Aubry, Craig Barton, Diane Chew, John Czajkowski, Rita Edwards, Michael Evans, Joan Geller, Tara Gomez, Carmella Granado, Rebel Holiday, Patti Holland, Bill Hughes, Yris Kayser, Kanu Kogod, Ellen Marshall, John McAuley, Karen McKay, Beth Meininger, Laura Mendelow, Ellen Moran, Nancy Nicholson, Tiza Pyle, Paula Richardson, Melinda Sinclair, Linda Noble Topf, T. Waldmann-Williams, and Harold Weinstein.

About the Author

Marilee Adams, Ph.D. is the founder and president of the Inquiry Institute and the originator of Question Thinking™. As a thought leader, consultant, executive coach, facilitator, and professional speaker for some of the world's leading companies, Marilee is often referred to as the Chief Question Officer. Her work sets the standard for transforming the spirit of inquiry into practical, powerful and user-friendly questioning skills and tools that are used throughout the world.

In her consulting practice, Marilee has witnessed the transformative power of Question Thinking for individuals, leaders, teams, organizations, and communities. This includes Fortune 100 companies, Lockheed Martin, Johnson & Johnson, Siemens Building Technologies, and DHL; the National Defense University and NASA Goddard in the Federal Government; hospitals such as Toronto General hospital; and national non-profit organizations the American Society of Training and Development, the Girl Scouts of America, and the Brookings Institution.

Before turning her attention to the world of business and organizational effectiveness, Marilee was a psychotherapist for more than twenty-five years, facilitating individuals, couples, and families in using thoughtful inquiry to create remarkable new possibilities for themselves. She also expresses her passion, commitment, and belief in the benefits of Learner inquiry through the Thoughtful Citizenship Project she founded as an initiative of the Inquiry Institute.

Marilee's first book, *The Art of the Question: a Guide to Short-Term Question-Centered Therapy* (John Wiley & Sons, 1998) was lauded as a "seminal and breakthrough contribution to the field of psychotherapy." The Question Thinking work at the core of the story in *Change Your Questions* is based on proven principles and research, described in that book, about how people think, feel, behave, and change.

Marilee has contributed book chapters on Question Thinking to *Action Learning and Its Applications* and to *Positively M.A.D.: Making a Difference in Your Organizations, Communities, and the World*. She co-authored, with Marge

Schiller, Ph.D. and David Cooperrider, Ph.D., a chapter for *Advances in Appreciative Inquiry, Vol. I.* She has also published articles on the expert use of questions in coaching, business, relationships, and organizational transformation. Marilee earned her Ph.D. in Clinical Psychology from the Fielding Graduate Institute, her Master's Degree in Social Work from Virginia Commonwealth University, is adjunct faculty for the Adler Institute of Coaching in Canada and lectures at Columbia University Teacher's College.

Marilee is a member of the Core Faculty, Certificates in Leadership Coaching, which is co-sponsored by Adler International Learning and the Ontario Institute for Studies in Education of the University of Toronto. She is also affiliated with Columbia University's Learning & Leadership (L&L) Group at Teachers College and is a member of the Berrett-Koehler Author Co-op Board.

Marilee and her husband, artist Ed Adams, live in the river town and arts community of Lambertville, New Jersey. She welcomes your correspondence at Choice@ InquiryInstitute.com.

Inquiry Institute

The Inquiry Institute is dedicated to bringing the benefits of Question Thinking and Learner Living to individuals, teams, organizations, families, communities, and society at large. Please visit our website to learn about:

- Question Thinking Workshops and Certification Programs
- Executive coaching and coach training
- Leadership, executive, and team development
- Creative and stategic thinking and innovation programs
- Digital resources and web-enhanced learning programs
- Discussion groups and active learning community
- Choice Map—a free color copy is available to download, which you can also forward to your friends and colleagues

Marilee Adams is available for keynote presentations and workshops (on-site and teleconference), leadership retreats, QStrategy, consulting, and executive coaching.

A request for you: We're eager to receive your success stories and questions. Please be in touch!

Inquiry Institute
10 York Street, P.O. Box 339
Lambertville, New Jersey 08530-3204
Phone: 800-250-7823

www.InquiryInstitute.com

Email: Choice@InquiryInstitute.com

THE **ASTD** MISSION:

Through exceptional learning and performance, we create a world that works better.

The American Society for Training & Development provides world-class professional development opportunities, content, networking, and resources for workplace learning and performance professionals.

Dedicated to helping members increase their relevance, enhance their skills, and align learning to business results, ASTD sets the standard for best practices within the profession.

The society is recognized for shaping global discussions on workforce development and providing the tools to demonstrate the impact of learning on the organizational bottom line. ASTD represents the profession's interests to corporate executives, policy makers, academic leaders, small business owners, and consultants through world-class content, convening opportunities, professional development, and awards and recognition.

Resources
- *T+D (Training + Development)* Magazine
- ASTD Press
- Industry Newsletters
- Research and Benchmarking
- Representation to Policy Makers

Networking
- Local Chapters
- Online Communities
- ASTD Connect
- Benchmarking Forum
- Learning Executives Network

Professional Development
- Certificate Programs
- Conferences and Workshops
- Online Learning
- CPLP™ Certification Through the ASTD Certification Institute
- Career Center and Job Bank

Awards and Best Practices
- ASTD BEST Awards
- Excellence in Practice Awards
- E-Learning Courseware Certification (ECC) Through the ASTD Certification Institute

Learn more about ASTD at www.astd.org.
1.800.628.2783 (U.S.) or 1.703.683.8100
customercare@astd.org

080615.31410

Berrett–Koehler
Publishers

Berrett-Koehler is an independent publisher dedicated to an ambitious mission: *Creating a World That Works for All.*

We believe that to truly create a better world, action is needed at all levels—individual, organizational, and societal. At the individual level, our publications help people align their lives with their values and with their aspirations for a better world. At the organizational level, our publications promote progressive leadership and management practices, socially responsible approaches to business, and humane and effective organizations. At the societal level, our publications advance social and economic justice, shared prosperity, sustainability, and new solutions to national and global issues.

A major theme of our publications is "Opening Up New Space." Berrett-Koehler titles challenge conventional thinking, introduce new ideas, and foster positive change. Their common quest is changing the underlying beliefs, mindsets, institutions, and structures that keep generating the same cycles of problems, no matter who our leaders are or what improvement programs we adopt.

We strive to practice what we preach—to operate our publishing company in line with the ideas in our books. At the core of our approach is stewardship, which we define as a deep sense of responsibility to administer the company for the benefit of all of our "stakeholder" groups: authors, customers, employees, investors, service providers, and the communities and environment around us.

We are grateful to the thousands of readers, authors, and other friends of the company who consider themselves to be part of the "BK Community." We hope that you, too, will join us in our mission.

A BK Life Book

This book is part of our BK Life series. BK Life books change people's lives. They help individuals improve their lives in ways that are beneficial for the families, organizations, communities, nations, and world in which they live and work. To find out more, visit **www.bk-life.com**.

Berrett–Koehler
Publishers

A community dedicated to creating
a world that works for all

Visit Our Website: www.bkconnection.com

Read book excerpts, see author videos and Internet movies, read
our authors' blogs, join discussion groups, download book apps, find
out about the BK Affiliate Network, browse subject-area libraries of
books, get special discounts, and more!

Subscribe to Our Free E-Newsletter, the *BK Communiqué*

Be the first to hear about new publications, special discount offers,
exclusive articles, news about bestsellers, and more! Get on the list
for our free e-newsletter by going to **www.bkconnection.com**.

Get Quantity Discounts

Berrett-Koehler books are available at quantity discounts for orders
of ten or more copies. Please call us toll-free at (800) 929-2929 or
email us at bkp.orders@aidcvt.com.

Join the BK Community

BKcommunity.com is a virtual meeting place where people from
around the world can engage with kindred spirits to create a world
that works for all. **BKcommunity.com** members may create their own
profiles, blog, start and participate in forums and discussion groups,
post photos and videos, answer surveys, announce and register for
upcoming events, and chat with others online in real time. Please join
the conversation!

MIX
From responsible
sources
FSC
www.fsc.org
FSC® C113845